GW01445347

Saving Planet Earth

A Christian Response

Colin A. Russell

Authentic

MILTON KEYNES • COLORADO SPRINGS • HYDERABAD

14 13 12 11 10 09 08   7 6 5 4 3 2 1

First published 2008 by Authentic Media
9 Holdom Avenue, Bletchley, Milton Keynes, Bucks, MK1 1QR, UK
1820 Jet Stream Drive, Colorado Springs, CO 80921, USA
OM Authentic Media, Medchal Road, Jeedimetla Village,
Secunderabad 500 055, A.P., India

www.authenticmedia.co.uk

Authentic Media is a division of IBS-STL U.K., limited by guarantee, with its
Registered Office at Kingstown Broadway, Carlisle, Cumbria CA3 0HA.
Registered in England and Wales No. 1216232. Registered charity 270162

British Library Cataloguing in Publication Data
A catalogue record for this book is available from the British Library

ISBN 978-1-85078-771-6

Cover design by fourninezero design.
Typeset by Waverley Typesetters, Fakenham
Print Management by Adare
Printed and bound in Great Britain by J.H. Haynes & Co., Sparkford

Contents

List of Illustrations

Preface

This book is intended for ordinary, busy people who are not experts. I hope it may be useful for church members who are newly aware of the environment but get little chance to see where their faith fits in. It is written from a Christian viewpoint and the authority of the Bible is taken for granted, as it should be for all the Christian church. However, I'd be happy if someone accused me of being an evangelical!

In many ways this is a 'first' for me. I happen to be an academic and usually write fairly academic books. This is not one of them, and you won't find the usual academic apparatus, like lots of footnotes, great book lists and so on. There *is* a list of books at the end, but it is not in any way the usual comprehensive bibliography. I thought it best just to provide a list that may prove useful for readers who want information that is accurate and expands what is written here. Similarly, the short list of addresses is far from complete but represents just a few of the organizations that I have found helpful.

I have tried hard to avoid an 'academic' style of writing, and to write a book that may even be readable! Forgive me if I've failed, and excuse my lapses as the habits of a lifetime. You may, however, guess that I'm a scientist and have a strong commitment to science as well as to Christianity.

In this book on the environment I have deliberately avoided the well-known lobbyists including such groups as the Green Party and Friends of the Earth. Much of their work is admirable and I have gained from it. We agree on lots of things but not (I guess) on the specifically Christian approach that I have adopted here. Rather than cause any embarrassment, I decided to avoid bringing them into the discussion.

I'm sure you will appreciate that this is just one man's understanding of our position on the Earth. However, I am encouraged by my membership of the John Ray Initiative to know that I am not alone but share the beliefs of very distinguished scientists who are also committed Christians. I am grateful for their support, as for that of my wife Shirley who has been my sternest critic and made many helpful comments.

More specifically, I must also thank the following:

> Sir John Houghton and IPCC, for the graphs in Figures 8 and 9;
>
> Rt. Rev. Dr. N. T. Wright, Bishop of Durham, for the quotation on pages 89 and 90;
>
> editors of *Developments*, for the quotation on page 68;
>
> Christian Aid for the quotation on page 68;
>
> Prof. C. B. de Witt and Prof. R. J. Berry for the statements from the Evangelical Declaration on the Care of Creation (Appendix 1).

I am grateful for all the help from the publishers, most particularly from the editor James Davies.

The book goes out with the hope that many Christians will find it useful in helping them to understand the rapidly changing times in which we all now live.

COLIN A. RUSSELL

Chapter 1

Priorities for the planet: why bother?

You don't need me to tell you how much we all establish priorities for ourselves. The priorities may not always be obvious, of course, but they exist all the same. If I refuse to dig the garden and prefer to watch TV, play video games or just sit down with a book, I have clearly put the garden job low in my priority list. In fact, that is sometimes how it is! If I always play football when I could be at church my priorities would be clear (that is *not* true in my case!). And when food comes before exercise the same is true. But if someone asked us honestly to give a list of our priorities we might often be hard put to supply an answer – they are so much part of our 'second nature' that we don't always realize that they are there. In science, there always has to be a priority of fact over fancy, whether that is an old primeval myth or a sophisticated modern theory that has not been sufficiently tested. Even in the lab, it is sometimes possible to forget that.

Priority choice comes to everyone: atheist, Christian, Muslim or whatever. This has never been more true than when questions of the environment arise. Vast numbers of people simply shrug their shoulders and forget what's happening around them. For them, care of the planet is low in the priority list, lower (for example) than their wish to travel, to eat extravagantly or sometimes just to waste rather than conserve or recycle. Others in the Christian church may have worthy priorities like paying the minister, modernizing the services, paying for a new roof, supporting missionaries, training the youth, or even Bible study or evangelism. Below these – often far below – is the question of attending to our environment. When was the last time you heard a sermon on the subject? For many of us, this has never happened.

In this chapter, I want to ask why people avoid this subject. There seem to be at least four reasons, four stumbling blocks in the way of a deep concern for the planet on which we live: the subject is (1) depressing, (2) difficult, (3) demeaning or even (4) dangerous. So let's look at these objections and see if they really stand up.

Objection 1: It's a depressing subject!

You can say that again! Those of cheerful disposition naturally turn away from such topics as the pollution of air and water with lethal consequences for many, the terrible extinction of wildlife, and the prospect for our grandchildren of a climate too hot for survival. People who inhabit a low-lying land, like Bangladesh, face the additional prospect of such awful flooding that millions may lose their homes and livelihood. Add to all that the dangers of pollution, what someone has called 'the rape of the countryside' as it is progressively covered with concrete, and the holes in the protective ozone layer, and there you have a pretty miserable scenario. Some people can't bring themselves to face it. Their motto might be, 'Eat, drink and be merry, for tomorrow we die.'

The environment's made even more depressing for some of us by two other things. One is that we simply can't get away from it. For the last three or four years in Britain, this has increasingly become a theme for politicians, many of whom are genuinely concerned and want to do something about it. Others, no doubt, see it as a political bandwagon. For others, again, it may be a distraction from more pressing domestic or foreign policy decisions. Either way, it has now become politically fashionable to talk earnestly about the environment. All this is great stuff for the media who love nothing more than a big crisis, enlivened by confrontation between progressives and others. So our depression is made even worse by constant exposure – we become victims of overkill.

There's another reason, too. The world around us is rapidly changing, and the older we are the more we are aware of how extensive those changes are. That may strengthen our resolve to avoid the issue – it's too depressing to contemplate! Prophets of doom are always unpopular, and today they're not all Christians.

Interestingly, in my opinion the younger generation are less put off by environmental problems; after all, they have the most to lose if and when things go pear-shaped. A recent survey of children under 11 showed that their greatest anxiety for the future was not terrorism or war but the environment. They really wanted to do something about it. Depressing or not, for their sake none of us can dodge the issue indefinitely.

Christians have another reason for ignoring any depressing feelings they may have concerning our planet's future. Other things in our faith can depress and discourage us, but we are still prepared to deal with them. Human sin is about the most depressing thing around but that doesn't deter us from facing it, in ourselves and in others, for the Good News is that through Christ sin has ultimately been conquered. To take just one example, we don't read the book of Revelation to scare ourselves silly by frightful visions of seven-headed monsters. Instead we read it to encourage ourselves through the vision of the Lamb who has conquered by his blood and destroyed the power of sin and death. The depressing subject of sin makes us all the more eager to proclaim the gospel of him who is its conqueror.

We know, as Paul said, that '… the whole creation has been groaning as in the pains of childbirth right up to the present time' (Rom. 8:22). But our Sovereign and Saviour God is in control, so lift up your hearts and know that even the environment matters to him. It should therefore matter to you.

Objection 2: It's a difficult subject!

Again different groups will feel threatened to different degrees. If you left school more than 15 years ago you would probably have heard little of the problems facing our planet. You might well complain that, 'We never had to worry about the environment when I was young!' Terms like *sustainability, greenhouse effect, acid rain, biodiversity* and so on are all unfamiliar and do not resonate. I am reminded of an incident a few months ago – with a few members of my family, I was climbing a gentle slope in the Cumbrian hills when I heard behind me a loud snorting noise reminiscent of a muffled steam engine. It grew louder every moment. Glancing back I saw we were being followed by a young lady with a large and obviously unfit dog. Its eyes protruded like beans on stalks, its tongue seemed to extend a metre or two from its mouth, but the most striking effect was the sound of its very heavy panting. We stood aside to let them pass. The following brief conversation ensued.

> Me: 'Do go past; we're not in a hurry.'
> She: 'Thank you very much.'
> *(trying to make light conversation)* Me: 'Your dog sounds like I sometimes feel.'
> She: 'Oh, he's a very old dog!'

I could not understand why my family fell about laughing! Comparison with 'a very old dog' was certainly unintended but a timely warning none the less. Age comes to all of us and before we know it, perhaps new technology has left us behind. The exertion to catch up can well leave some of us panting. Not the least of our problems may be the sheer difficulty of grasping the new language.

Environmental terms are not usually hard to understand. In fact it is often not the ideas but the *words* that are fairly new. For example, the Victorians never talked about 'environment' but they often spoke of 'nature'. It is simply the material world around us. The Bible itself refers to 'the world' when it speaks of God's created things around us. The other 'difficult' words are all easy to explain, as I hope to demonstrate as you read on.

However, there is one thing that *will* be difficult: putting into practice what we discover to be our responsibility. Christians have less excuse than anyone else for dodging that kind of difficulty. Yet there remains another objection that may be put by Christians and non-Christians alike.

Objection 3: It's a demeaning subject!

This is the view that 'the Earth is made for humans so we are free to use it as we will'. Such an opinion dates back at least as far as the Roman poet Cicero, and is found in writing ever since. This was why many people (not necessarily churchgoers) were so opposed to Darwin. Their opposition was not on the basis of Scripture or theology but simply because the theory seemed to reduce man to the level of just another animal. It is well illustrated in the cartoon of an ape meeting a very surprised man at a party.

FIGURE 1. The ape at a party (*Punch* magazine)

A party-goer surprised by one guest!

In the same way, some feel humanity demeans itself by caring for rocks, air, water, plants and animals. For them, man is 'the king of creation'. If using creation for our own benefit means loss of animal species, pollution of rivers, destruction of forests, then it is just a tough choice we have to make. The captains and leaders of industry have always taken this view until recently. Only now has the rape of the Earth been on such a scale that even they are bound to sit up and take notice.

The great astronomer Copernicus believed the world was made 'for our sake'. One of the founders of modern science, Francis Bacon who lived in the 17th century, held that man was destined for the dominion of nature, 'to the glory of God and the relief of man's estate'. He did not say that 'anything goes' but one could be forgiven for supposing that he got very near to it.

It was this kind of belief that prompted an American historian, Lynn Townsend White, jun., to produce an essay in 1967 that stressed what a mess we had made of our world. He went on to suggest that Christianity itself was partly to blame, as Christians took the injunction of Genesis 1:28 as permission to do just about whatever they wanted to the natural world. Looking back, we can see that White was right to draw attention to our plight, but wrong to suppose that the faith of the Bible led to such abuse. In fact, the historical evidence now available suggests the opposite. But White's essay is still quoted in arguments against the Christian faith.

The force of his argument, that man must be master, still makes many people wonder whether any other course is not going to demean the 'special' status of man. Whether this comes from pagan or alleged Christian sources hardly matters. One emphasis of this book is that it can only be negated by a Christian affirmation that the Earth is not ours but the Lord's.

Objection 4: It's a dangerous subject!

The final objection is of a very different kind. It can be a huge problem for some Christians but is not likely to deter others who won't need to read any more of this chapter. Perhaps the commonest objection by Christians to caring for our planet is expressed in the words 'It's not in the Bible.' That suggests that we don't need to bother with it – it would be a dangerous distraction – as the word 'environment' is not in any biblical concordance. However, the challenge to care for God's creation *is* in the Bible, as the rest of this book will try to show. So please suspend judgement on this one!

Some Christians are generally suspicious of novelties, with due reason. They may complain, 'It's just a modern fad'. In fact, they are quite wrong, for Christians down the ages have shown an awareness of the need to care for God's world. To mention a single example, the great John Calvin once wrote, 'The earth was given to man, with this condition, that he should occupy himself in its cultivation', and much else in this vein, as we shall see later. What is novel is not the call to be concerned but rather the new perils that our forefathers never dreamt of. Our environment faces new threats and there is a new awareness of their magnitude. So our situation is new, but not to be ignored for that reason. It is rather like that of slavery in the early 19th century – the church took over 18 centuries to realize that slavery was incompatible with biblical teaching on equality, and was eventually abolished when external pressures (political in this case) made it possible for a group of Christians to take action. As it happened, this group was composed of evangelicals, perhaps more open than others to biblical imperatives. The light shining from God's Word was as applicable to

19th-century slavery abolitionists as it may prove to be for 21st-century pioneers in environmental action.

A further objection, that it is dangerous to become involved in the care of our planet, is sometimes put like this: 'You are playing into the hands of new age movements'. 'New agers' tend to care for the Earth because it (or 'she' as they might say) is alive, even divine. Such beliefs are utterly at variance with Scripture which proclaims the world and the universe as entities created by God, and never to be identified with him. These beliefs go back to Babylonian and Egyptian times. Genesis chapters 1–2 can be seen as a trumpet-call to abandon them and to see the Earth as a creation of the all powerful God. It is obvious that Christians can have no truck with such heresies. We are right to be suspicious of an agenda that seems to derive from them. In fact, today's call for environmental action does not depend at all on pre-Christian myths. Once again I would ask you to wait until later chapters for further discussion of this matter.

The final objection that it is dangerous to focus on the environment is by far the most telling. We can be deflected from our real task: proclamation of the Good News. Some often say, 'I'd rather preach the gospel', or 'We're here to save souls not the planet.' That is doubtless one reason why so few sermons are preached on the topic. Evangelicals and charismatics might seem to be the most likely groups to encourage such an attitude. A question that bothered me for ages was 'Are they right?'

Of course, it is true that recycling tin cans will not save a soul. Diminishing global warming will do nothing to reduce the heat of God's anger against sin. No amount of environmental activity can ever make a man or woman right before God. That alone comes through the cross.

We can also think of 'saving the earth' as dangerous in another sense. It may distract us from eagerly expecting the return of Jesus Christ. When (not if) this happens He will begin to transform our planet into something infinitely better, to 'save' it in a profound sense, and to create a new Heaven and Earth. Why should we bother? The simple answer is that, as He said in several parables, the returning Bridegroom expects the waiting bridesmaids to be ready, the returning Landlord to have his servants work as efficiently as possible.

Care of planet Earth can never be the *heart* of the gospel. But then that is true of many other good activities like care of the sick, the poor and the needy. However, it may be that this is *part* of the gospel – as I hope to show later. If so, it is not a matter of *either* preaching the cross *rather than* tending the planet. It is not *either or* it is *both and*. There are potent reasons for believing this, and it is interesting that much of the recent Christian impetus for concern comes from the evangelical wing of the church. Why this should be so we will discuss later.

In 1994, a group of leaders produced an Evangelical Declaration on the Care of Creation. It begins with words from Psalm 24: 'The earth is the Lord's, and the fullness thereof', and concludes with this affirmation: 'knowing that until Christ returns to reconcile all things, we are called to be faithful stewards of God's good garden, our earthly home' (R. J. Berry (ed.), *The Care of Creation*, IVP, Leicester, 2000, pp. 17–22) (see Appendix 1).

So is it dangerous for Christians to try to clean up the environment? Only if that activity distracts us from the rest of the gospel. It is just as dangerous to neglect this part of the gospel as it is to pick and choose other parts.

Chapter 2

Our home in space

The Earth, our home, is undoubtedly a wonderful place. You don't have to be a poet or an artist to recognize that! If you happen to have some sympathy for what artists and poets do, you may well appreciate the wonderful things they see around them: scenes of mountain and lake, flowers in close-up, all kinds of animal life, the soaring of an eagle, the intricacies of a single snowflake and (of course) the inevitable sunsets. But it is when we experience these things for ourselves that they really impress us. When I was in New Zealand, I went for a walk one evening in the country. Looking up at the night sky, at the stars that form the Southern Cross high in the sky, and hundreds of other stars in view, I could only gaze and wonder at the staggering beauty of it all, and my heart was lifted to its Creator. It wasn't so much 'morning by morning' as 'evening by evening' that 'new beauties I see'! Hymn writers have made much of the sheer loveliness of our home in space, from 'All things bright and beautiful' to many modern songs. If you get a chance to hear John Rutter's setting of 'For the beauty of the earth' you will find timeless words sung to a haunting new tune.

Planet Earth is special

However, it is not only poets, artists and musicians that can help us appreciate our planet. That privilege also falls to scientists. Mention of such people may cause some Christians to reach for their guns (metaphorically). But that is entirely unnecessary, as science has long been an ally to the faith. When it emerged in its modern form about 400 years ago, its great inspiration was the Bible, and nearly all the early scientists were firm believers. Even problem incidents have done little to disturb the alliance, as when Galileo was forced to recant his scientific views by the Roman Catholic Inquisition in the 17th century, or when Darwin was criticized by a few Victorian Christians for daring to suppose that human bodies were related to those of animals. Today, hundreds of effective scientists own Jesus as Lord. In fact, the insights of modern science show far more of the wonders of the Earth than we could possibly have known about otherwise.

In the next few pages I want to share with you just a tiny fragment of what science has disclosed about the marvels of planet Earth. David Attenborough's TV series has done a great service in helping us to appreciate the wonders of life on Earth. The photography is breathtaking, and the biology is right up to date. One is reminded of insect-eating flowers, of birds, whales and fish travelling thousands of miles each year, of animals surviving high in the rain forests, of the incredible courtship rituals of exotic birds, and so on. But it would be impertinent of me to add to what he has shown us of the living world. Instead let me focus on some other aspects of our planet.

Perhaps the chief thing to say is that planet Earth is wonderfully adapted to the needs of the human race, far more so than was ever realized by people in ancient times. Think of such a simple thing as the air we breathe. Most people know that it's a mixture of two gases, oxygen and nitrogen (in a proportion of about 1 to 4). Oxygen is what we need in order to survive: when we breathe it in we expel carbon dioxide which takes up less than 1 per cent of the air. This is because it is turned back into oxygen by some plants and the amount in our atmosphere has been pretty constant since measurements began. Very recently it has risen, but the astonishing thing about air is that until now its composition has been just right for us: too much oxygen and we'd all catch fire, too little and we'd suffocate.

There is another form of oxygen called ozone. This is quite nasty stuff to have around, and when cars emit it in badly-tuned engines we have a right to complain. However, about 17 miles above the earth's surface, where we can't possibly breathe it in, there is a belt of ozone encircling our planet. No one knew it was there until fairly recently and in our own day it has been discovered that, in places like Antarctica, it has developed several 'holes'. We now know this is bad news, because the ozone layer has hitherto given us an invisible shield against much of the dangerous radiation bombarding us from space. Without its protection we would be vulnerable to all kinds of skin cancer and the human race probably would not have survived. That is why 'holes' in the ozone layer are so dangerous (more on this later). So far as we know, we are the only planet to have this remarkable shield in place.

Another totally amazing feature is water, billions of tons of it. We know of no other planet *in our solar system* where this is true, and yet without it we simply would not be here. It is also possible that water might exist elsewhere in the universe, but that is only *one* of the many conditions for life. Recently, it has been suggested, for example, that a planet called GLIESE, 581 c, associated with a red star far away from our solar system, *might* have the right conditions for liquid water to exist on its surface. We shall have to wait and see.

On Earth, we find water everywhere and take it totally for granted, though in fact it is remarkable in so many ways that it can truly be called 'unique'. Here are some of the ways in which water differs from almost every other liquid and these properties all help to make our life possible.

First, most liquids contract when you cool them – in other words, the solid form of the substance does not float on the liquid form because it is more dense. However, when you get down to about 4°C, water starts to expand. This means that very cold water and ice are less dense than the water they came from and therefore *ice floats*. Hence, you have icebergs, but not the prospect of a sea freezing from the bottom upwards. If water froze from the bottom upwards, like virtually every other liquid, this would eliminate fish life and much else besides. Also, the expansion on freezing means that, in a hard frost, water in rocks will expand and crack the rocks (just as it used to do to lead pipes). Thus the soil we till in gardening, and the whole surface of the earth, is changed by frost. Hardly any other substance behaves like this.

There is more. Water takes an awful lot of heat to raise its temperature and still more to bring it to the boil. Hence we don't have violent changes in earth's water as the days get hotter. Water, as people say, 'keeps its heat' a long time (which is why it is best to be careful when eating hot jam tarts!). So we don't have sudden rushes of temperature up and down as the air temperature changes – life would not tolerate that. The technical way of talking about these phenomena is that water has high heat capacity and high latent heat. No other common liquid even gets close to water's qualities.

Then again, water will dissolve so many things. These include gases like CO_2 which enable water to dissolve even more, like limestone rocks. The effect on our landscape is enormous, but even more important is the fact that water is the basic fluid of our bodies, and the bodies of all living creatures. It transports chemicals within cells and from one cell to another and enables myriads of complex chemical reactions to take place whenever we breathe, eat, move a muscle or even sleep. If the Earth's temperature was less than 0°C or above 100°C none of this would be possible!

Water is a compound of hydrogen and oxygen, with the most famous formula in the world H_2O. Chemists now begin to understand why it is so special, one reason being that it readily gives rise to hydrogen ions (positively charged hydrogen atoms, also known as protons). It is these which travel about our cells, sometimes hopping over long chains of water molecules in a way that nothing else ever can. All of life's processes involve water, the most abundant liquid on Earth. One scientist wrote recently that the ingenuity that life displays in shepherding protons is breathtaking. Precisely. Or one might prefer to ascribe that ingenuity to God.

In a chemistry lecture I gave years ago on oxygen and its compounds, I was astounded to have an interruption from the floor. Students just didn't do that kind of thing in those days. I had been talking simply as a chemist about this remarkable substance when a student stood up and said, 'Sir [that's what they used to call you years ago!] you almost make me believe in a God.' I have to say I was quite nonplussed; I had not been trying to argue for the existence of God, though I gladly admitted that I did believe in him. It was simply that the facts told their own story.

The wonders of our planet for life have long been used as an argument for a Designer; they called that 'Natural

theology'. Michael Green once gave an illustration
something like this: imagine you are playing a giant game
of Scrabble, with many thousand pieces. You leave the
room and return to find someone has upset the game, and
instead of loose pieces on the floor you discover an *Oxford
English Dictionary*. Did the random letters just happen to
land in all the right places, or was there a designing mind
behind the book? Back in 1800, William Paley used the same
kind of argument about the universe. He compared it to a
watch picked up from a heath. After a lengthy examination
he concludes the watch had not always been there, it had
not been (like a heap of stones) a random collection of
objects, but was the result of immensely careful design.
Can you believe that planet Earth is anything else? I have
to say that, logically, you cannot *prove* God that way or any
other, but the evidence is immensely *suggestive*. Once you
believe in him, the chemistry of Earth begins to make a
whole lot more sense.

Nowadays, it is fashionable to speak of the universe
as though it had been designed for man, the so-called
Anthropic Principle. That's often how it seems when
you look at it through a scientist's eyes. Many religious
people, not just Christians, would agree. In the Bible, there
are many verses that speak of man as the peak of God's
creation and of everything else made for his benefit. For
example, Psalm 65:9–13:

> You care for the land and water it; you enrich it abundantly.
> The streams of God are filled with water to provide the
> people with grain, for so you have ordained it. You drench
> its furrows and level its ridges; you soften it with showers
> and bless its crops. You crown the year with your bounty,
> and your carts overflow with abundance.
>
> The grasslands of the desert overflow; the hills are clothed
> with gladness. The meadows are covered with flocks and

the valleys are mantled with grain; they shout for joy and sing.

Note especially the second sentence. There is no doubt that the Bible concurs with at least part of the Anthropic Principle, but ascribes it fundamentally to our Creator. But that, as we shall see, is only half the story.

One last thing about the science of planet Earth. Today many people are worried about how tiny we are, alone in a vast space filled with millions of stars. In the light of modern cosmology, we need be neither surprised nor worried. Life, as we know it, depends on a large number of chemical elements such as hydrogen, oxygen, nitrogen, phosphorus and (especially) carbon. Currently, the scientific evidence suggests that these have all been made from something much simpler since the universe began – in other words since God set the whole thing in motion. But this synthesis takes a very long time, millions of years in fact. During that period, the universe has been expanding at a colossal rate, and that is why it is so big today and we are just a tiny part of it. The evidence really does suggest that the 'Big Bang' took place nearly 14,000 million years ago. If so, it took our Creator nearly all that time to produce such a complicated thing as the human body, and rather less than that to make planet Earth. The oldest rock that has been found so far is 4,000 million years old.

Some Christians are worried by these figures, needlessly I believe. Scientists like other human beings may make mistakes but it is hardly likely that they are greatly in error on this subject. If they are wrong, planet Earth is nothing like so wonderful a place as I have portrayed it! But it is still our home and worthy to be loved and cared for.

Meanwhile most of us wonder whether or not we are alone in such a vast space. Is life out there on some other planet? So far there has been no evidence for any such thing, but we must be cautious and not be too upset if we find it. How many more civilizations are there waiting to be found by *Starship Enterprise*? The honest answer is that we don't know, but equally we don't *need* to know. There are, however, two very important things about our own planet that we dare not overlook. The first of these was aptly named by C. S. Lewis in an early piece of science fiction that he wrote back in 1938. He called Earth the 'silent planet', and this is why he did so.

Planet Earth is spoiled

In Lewis' novel *Out of the Silent Planet*, a human being called Ransom finds himself on a journey to another planet, Mars. He discovers that the Earth that he has just left is strangely incommunicado with the rest of the universe. It is, in his story, isolated from everything else by a corruption called sin. He calls it 'The silent planet'. That is why in general Lewis was against human travel into space, for fear that we should bring with us 'the vomit of our own corruption'.

It's a fanciful tale, but a good example of quite early space fiction. Yet the underlying idea that there is something deeply wrong with Earth, and that this springs from human sinfulness, is soundly biblical. In a word, Earth is where sin reigns; and has been suffering ever since that process began. The traumas of the world today cry out for some explanation, and for that there is nowhere better to turn than the first few chapters of the Bible: Genesis 1–3 and onwards.

Here is celebrated the very first act of creation by Almighty God. The perfection of his handiwork, explored by science, is repeated again and again in the first chapter: 'God saw that it was good'. Beauty and magnificence are all around, a man appears and is given a wife. They enjoy the views, they enjoy food and they enjoy sex.

Then catastrophe occurs and the blissful days are over. Adam and Eve are cast out of the beautiful garden called Eden, or Paradise, and find the Earth they will now inhabit has changed almost beyond recognition. It is not long before jealousy, murder and vengeance stalk the land, work becomes back-breaking and, as the human race multiplies, the Iron Age is upon them, men make tools and play instruments, but wickedness increases to such a point that direct judgement from God comes down in a one-off natural disaster known as the Flood.

What then went wrong? Our first ancestors made a mistake not about an 'apple' but about the place of God in their lives. At first they merely questioned his *word*: 'Did God really say?' (Gen. 3:1), but then they spurned his *authority* and disobeyed him. Poets from John Milton onwards have written vast works about Paradise Lost, theologians have argued about 'original sin', and young people today have tried to marry the theology and the science. But when it comes down to it, *this is the story of you and me*. Our sin and our subsequent problems stem from simply putting ourselves before God.

The big question is whether the material planet has been spoilt. It certainly looks as though it has. Many a mother will be able to appreciate Paul's words: 'We know that the whole creation has been groaning as in the pains of childbirth right up to the present time' (Rom. 8:22). In the story of the fall Adam, it is told: '... Cursed is the ground because of you; through painful toil you will eat of it all the days of your life. It will produce thorns and thistles for you, and you will eat the plants of the field. By the sweat of your brow you will eat your food until you return to the ground, since from it you were taken; for dust you are and to dust you will return' (Gen. 3:17–19). Many a toiling gardener would echo that one!

So we have tsunamis, earthquakes and other 'natural disasters' that so afflict our world. Just what is the connection between human sin and a damaged planet is not made clear.

Sometimes of course, human sin directly leads to suffering, as when a disobedient child experiments with live electric wires. The growth of AIDS, the effects of smoking, death through drunken driving, etc. are often linked to human failures. But we must be careful. When Jesus was on Earth he was told of various disasters, one of which was the collapse of a tower, killing 18 persons. He warned his disciples to be very sparing of their judgement of others: '… those eighteen who died when the tower in Siloam fell on them – do you think they were more guilty than all the others living in Jerusalem? I tell you, no! But unless you repent, you too will all perish' (Luke 13:4,5).

Sadly, this specially favoured planet has become silent with sorrow and destruction. Fortunately, it is also the place where our deliverance has begun.

Planet Earth is saveable

Such reflections may cause despair for our environment and for anything else, and we could fall into a deep pessimism. If things are really that bad, what hope is there? Politicians may urge us to turn off taps, travel on foot and do all sorts of other good things for the environment, but at the end of the day are they likely to be successful? Experience suggests that this will not be the case, unless politics can be supported by something else.

This book tries to argue that in the Christian faith there is hope – real, solid hope – for the world, and that this involves our planet in an amazing way. Unlike the time when our troubles began, or even unlike the origin of our Earth, we can date the start of this process with astonishing precision. Thanks to all kinds of analysis of planetary movements, ancient records and much else, the date is probably somewhere between 9 March and 4 May 5 BC. In other words, it is the birth of a baby in an obscure town in Palestine, about five years earlier than traditional calendars might suggest.

The event is of course celebrated at Christmas, and the baby was Jesus Christ. The great theme of Christianity is that this child was God-made-man, something that normal science cannot comprehend because, however you look at it, this was not a 'normal' event. Here was God the Creator taking upon himself the form of one of his creatures, a human form. Here the author of this mighty universe came to rescue a tiny planet and those who live upon it. Planet Earth was to become the stage for the most amazing drama ever to be seen, probably in the entire vast universe.

So Earth is where God became man in Jesus, who 'did not consider equality with God something to be grasped, but made himself nothing, taking the very nature of a servant, being made in human likeness' (Phil. 2:6,7). If this is true then we his followers should have (among other things) the humility *we* need to clean up our environment. But there is much more to it than that. This celestial visitor to our planet Earth was not just giving us an example. He was wrestling with forces far beyond our control. We see this particularly in the writings of the Apostle John.

John, more often than the other Gospel writers, often uses the Greek word 'cosmos' for our world. Of Jesus, he said 'the world was made by him' (John 1:10). Sometimes he means the planet plus its inhabitants (as in John 3:16: 'God so loved the world that he gave his one and only Son, that whoever believes in him shall not perish but have eternal life'). But sometimes he means this planet as opposed to the rest of the universe. On several occasions he indicates that, underneath all our own corruption and sin, lurks a more sinister power, which he calls 'the prince of this world'. This is the power that Jesus has come to defeat (John 14:30), which will be driven out (12:31) and condemned (16:11).

That victory was gloriously accomplished by his death and resurrection. At the cross, he died to pay the price of our sin. Graham Kendrick's song 'The Servant King' paints the incredible paradox of the very hands that created our planet and universe being willingly nailed to a cross. Such was the drama played out on our planet. But it did not end there.

On the third day, his body emerged from the dark tomb and the first Christians discovered to their utter amazement that Jesus was once again alive! The resurrection of Christ, though quite outside the normal experience of science, has been described by one historian as 'the best attested fact in history'. Indeed, the evidence now available to us has converted many an honest sceptic. Its theological implications are enormous, and the following two simple facts are incontestable. First, the living presence of Jesus in his followers means that the awful problems of suffering and pain take on a wholly new meaning; he is with his disciples in their pain, sharing it with them and enabling them to cope, and he also brings good out of evil (just as he did at the cross). Second, the presence of the risen Christ among his people ever since has enabled them to accomplish so much that would otherwise have been impossibly difficult for them. It means that, if his ideals are followed, and his power used by his disciples, then the world can be saved and hope is not dead. Paul writes of an even greater hope: 'I consider that our present sufferings are not worth comparing with the glory that will be revealed in us. The creation waits in eager expectation for the sons of God to be revealed' (Rom. 8:18,19).

One last point is that some have felt that this uniqueness of planet Earth means that life in outer space must be impossible. Otherwise there would be countless other incarnations and crucifixions.

There are several fallacies there. First, it does not follow that life in another planet would be sentient, i.e. capable of feeling and knowing. It could be as simple as a one-celled organism or as complex as a cabbage. In neither case would any redemption be needed. However, such life might just possibly be able to know and to communicate with us. But it does not follow that such sentient life forms had to be 'saved' in any sense.

Even if something like sentient life does exist elsewhere it may not be anything like ours, and it may not have taken the fateful step of sinning. And even if, in the last and worst scenario, it had sinned like us, who is to say that Almighty God has to use the same methods as he has with the human race?

If money is to be spent on searching space for signs of life, that must be a political and not a religious decision. We may well ask if that is the best use of resources, but we should never bother for one instant whether it might destroy our faith. On possibilities of other life in space, the Bible is naturally and rightly silent. We can never know the answers and (as we said earlier) we do not need to know. The God who loved us sufficiently to send his Son into our fallen world can be trusted with anything.

So, we live on a planet that has so much going for it, is in a dreadful mess but has been potentially set free by the coming of Jesus Christ. If that is all true, what kind of a mess do we face, and why do people say the Earth is in danger? Three answers will appear in the next three chapters. Read on!

Chapter 3

A polluted planet

Pollution is not a new problem to our planet, though it is only in the last 40 or so years that people have become excited about it. It's mentioned a few times in the Old Testament, though generally God was more concerned with his people's inward state than their environments, warning them not to pollute ('defile') themselves through the worship of images and lots of other evils. As the prophet said, 'The land you are entering to possess is a land polluted by the corruption of its peoples' (Ezra 9:11).

We shall see later that there are potent spiritual reasons for getting rid of the material pollution that threatens us, but our concern for now is just what the problem is, and what simple measures can be taken against it.

Our modern concern goes back to the early 1960s. In 1962, Rachel Carson produced a book called *Silent Spring* which sent alarm bells ringing all over the Western world. Many familiar songbirds were being found dead or injured and she imagined one year when their spring chorus would be absent; then it would be a truly silent spring. The culprit was a chemical called DDT, which had been widely used to kill insects that threatened to destroy much-needed crops. It was very effective but unfortunately was absorbed by birds that ate the affected insects and the poison remained in their bodies, leading to a slow death. Rachel Carson's campaign called for elimination of all such 'chemical' pesticides. It was remarkably successful in Europe and America, where DDT was banned, even though it was later shown to have been highly beneficial in other places by destroying the mosquitoes that carried the tropical disease malaria. DDT is still used in 25 countries, including South Africa. In 2006/7, the World Health Organization has overruled the US ban and has, for example, approved the use of DDT in walls and crevices. Here it cannot reach birds, animals or humans (unless they start to lick the walls!).

Recent work has shown that it can be slowly removed from the soil by small amounts of seaweed, so even here there is hope. Ever since the 1960s there has been a lively debate over the rights and wrongs of using artificial chemicals in agriculture. It's a long and complicated story but marked a new misunderstanding of environmental pollution. What may seem to pollute the planet may be shown to cause more good than harm, and vice versa. We need to be constantly vigilant on this score.

How then is our planet polluted and do we need to do anything about it? Let's look at a few cases.

Polluted land

There was once an Old Testament injunction, 'Do not pollute the land where you are' (Num. 35:33) and that has been relevant ever since. A human tendency to dump unwanted things anywhere on land within reach has long been cause for complaint. Let me give you one example out of many.

Leather-makers were notorious for dumping. They took animal carcases when the butchers had finished with them, but needed only the skins for their product.

Everything else (horns, hooves, etc.) was just dumped, often left for months on end. The stench made leather-makers very unpopular and all over England laws were passed in the 16th century compelling them to clear the land or face prosecution. Not all land pollution was as smelly as that, but as time wore on and city populations increased a new menace emerged in the form of raw sewage. One method of disposal was for farmers to spread it on their land as fertilizer. This led one optimist to suggest it produced 'a transformation more beautiful than any known to pantomime. Leaves are spreading upwards, roots are spreading outwards . . .'! That at least was an early effort to convert a nuisance to a benefit, and in a much modified form is still used today.

But we mustn't be hard on leather-makers. Industrial residues litter the countryside, though they are often not visible. Boreholes on a new building site can often indicate what industry was there many years earlier. In Cornwall, the sites of old tin-works have a far higher percentage of arsenic than anywhere else in the UK (sometimes over 60 times the average), on Tyneside there are still hillocks of waste sulphur from Victorian chemical works, and former lead mines in West Durham are littered with stacks of the toxic lead compounds. Throughout Britain, the relics of heavy industry lurk hidden beneath a thin layer of topsoil, and even the 'brown field' sites of so-called light industry, are usually unfit for cultivation. From abandoned cars littering the fields of Shetland (there is no disposal facility on the islands) to miles of concrete runways of disused airfields the story is the same. Our land is heavy with pollution.

Other examples of land pollution come from farming. The farmers' job has always been to provide humanity with food. The trouble is that they couldn't do it fast enough. The increasing population of the world made

FIGURE 2. Shetland notice: what to do with your waste

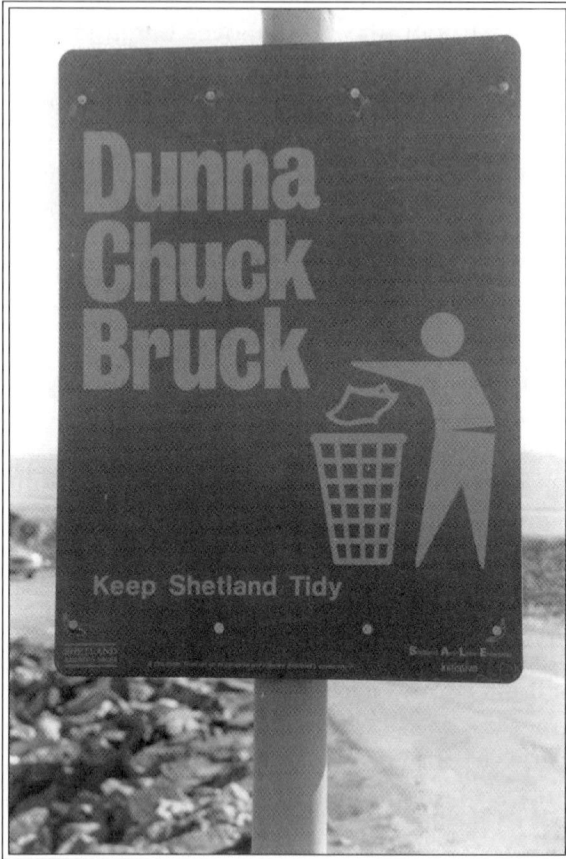

What Shetlanders should do with their rubbish ['bruck']

their task much more urgent. They were able to use artificial fertilizers with great success. The results were spectacular, and wheat production was dramatically increased. Today, worldwide crop production needs at least to double if starvation is to be eliminated and variations of these fertilizers are still needed.

However, not all necessary nutrients could be provided in this way, and there were other disadvantages, as when some of these added materials were washed into streams and rivers and ended up in drinking water (a bad thing). Some people regarded these chemicals as pollutants and natural manures were preferred. This led to what is mis-called 'organic farming' when no man-made chemicals are allowed to enter the environment. Unfortunately, this is much more expensive than other farming and may be able to cover only 15 per cent of the world's needs. 'Organic farming' is much more than avoiding artificial fertilizers, but it does seem to rely on a huge assumption, that 'nature's ways are best'. While that may sometimes be true, it has no support in the Bible whose authors, of course, knew nothing of 'chemicals'. We dare not make a matter of taste into a principle of theology!

If unwanted fertilizers really are a pollutant on our land, another area of agriculture rightly attracts much more suspicion. This relates to chemicals added to kill unwanted species, pesticides in general. If insects are the target, they are known as insecticides, if weeds they are called herbicides. This is where Rachel Carson was partly right: the DDT insecticide was wreaking havoc on wildlife. Since then many other substances have been shown to have all kinds of undesirable side effects. Apparently less nasty alternatives have been found, though 'organic farming' will not use them. However, the situation is that these chemicals that pollute our land are in fact vital to the survival of the human race.

Nevertheless we must be warned, since the case of DDT has much to teach us. It has been banned in America, and by last year (2007) the World Wide Fund for Nature has called for a 'global phase-out and total ban on production'. This reflects what is sometimes called 'the green orthodoxy', but it is far from certain that it is right. The biggest killer disease on our planet is malaria, probably responsible for nearly half the human deaths that have ever occurred. The malaria parasite is killed by DDT! Within a space of 25 years it is estimated that 1,000 million lives have been saved by the use of DDT. And a World Health Organization report said that 10 countries, previously ravaged by malaria, had been released by DDT from 'the angel of death'. Yet some people want to deprive African and other cultures of this life-saving chemical. It may not be true that 'environmentalism is a religion that has killed millions' (M. Crichton), but it is a fact that religious people generally may be sometimes inclined to jump on the green bandwagon without real knowledge of the facts. We must be warned!

At present we lose about 50 per cent of all crops grown through destruction by insects, about 70 per cent in the less developed world, and we need to double, not halve, production of our food! Just one example from thousands must suffice. In Ghana, the production of cocoa has increased by 300 per cent since the introduction of insecticides that eliminated the capsid bug which previously ate most of the crop.

In animal farming, the issues are similar. In order to increase the size of poultry it has been found that administration of certain antibiotics may do the trick. Accordingly, for many years a poultry feed was supplied which had antibiotics included. The problems arose when it was found that these antibiotics often survived the cooking process and therefore entered the food chain of human beings. This meant people ingested antibiotics when they didn't need them, and they developed a resistance to some of the 'super bugs' that they might later catch. Even life-saving antibiotics may be a pollutant of the Earth in the wrong place; their agricultural use has been largely banned.

In the 21st century, we are faced with two other terrible forms of land pollution. One is the mountain of domestic waste that comes from our dustbins. Only now are many local authorities seeking to reduce the problem by recycling; they deserve all our support (see also chapter 4).

The other modern example is pollution by concrete, where large areas of green countryside are being covered by new motorways and housing estates. These may both be needed, but the cost is high. Not only is there (in some people's eyes) visual pollution, but, much more important, there is a loss of grass and other vegetation that helps our planet to 'breathe'. Some of us can reduce this form of land pollution by cultivating the green areas of our gardens and not covering everything with concrete (or bricks or even wood). If you want to double the hard-standing for your car in the front garden – please think again!

Polluted water

Biblical writers were all too familiar with this type of pollution, and one made an unfavourable comparison between 'a muddied spring or a polluted well' and 'a righteous man who gives way to the wicked' (Prov. 25:26). For centuries, streams and rivers have been convenient places to dispose of everything from leather-makers' offal to modern industrial effluents. As industry thrived after about 1800, the problem became acute and our rivers became the sinks of society. Not only was their water undrinkable, but also the adjoining land shared in their contamination. In the 19th century, legislation was eventually put in place to keep our watercourses pure.

This was partly to placate the powerful fisheries lobby, who wished to protect the salmon they were trying to catch. The chemical factories that flourished in northern Britain poured dyestuffs, acids and alkalis into the rivers with little resistance from the government, and the gasworks springing up all over the country once disposed of their tar by similar means. Eventually rivers (though not estuaries) were protected by law in Britain and some other countries. One English chemist, consulted by a firm that wanted to dispose of a large amount of evil-smelling sludge, gave the astonishing advice to take the waste in small boats 'and throw it into the Severn'!

In Britain and many other European countries there was an even worse kind of water-pollution. As big towns developed, there was no way of disposing of sewage in the simple earth closets in rural areas. In time, it was channelled into the very rivers from which drinking water was drawn. Time after time the towns were ravaged by plagues like cholera which were eventually shown to be water-borne diseases, nourished by the sewage arrangements of the time. In 1855, London was enveloped by the 'Great Stink' which resulted from a foul-smelling fog over the River Thames. The scientist Michael Faraday took a trip down the river and found it so polluted that the lower half of a card dropped in edgeways became invisible before the top was in the water! The 'Great Stink' became the subject of vigorous discussion in the pages of *The Times*.

Eventually the cause of disease was traced to water-borne particles and any number of chemists, distinguished and otherwise, were put to work to discover when water could be safely drunk. One of them was Edward Frankland whose methods of analysis just saved the day for great cities like London. It was science that staved off epidemics of unbelievable proportions and led (eventually) to a vast

FIGURE 3. Faraday on the Thames (*Punch* magazine, 1855)

FARADAY GIVING HIS CARD TO FATHER THAMES;

And we hope the Dirty Fellow will consult the learned Professor.

Pollution of the Thames

reduction in water-borne pollution generally. We can only be grateful.

Of course these examples come from the UK. If we look further afield the situation seems to be very different. The developing world does not have our problems of intensive farming (unless for international supermarkets) or concentrated industry. Its chief pollution comes from water instead. To mention one particularly nasty substance again, arsenic occurs in about 30 per cent of the wells registered in Bangladesh and action is being taken first of all to identify the polluted wells, and then to find means of mitigating its effects. Similar problems exist elsewhere in Asia, e.g. in northern India.

One of the Millennium Goals (no. 7) of Britain's Department for International Development is to halve the proportion of people worldwide who have no access to safe drinking water and sanitation by 2025. That is a huge task but one surely to be welcomed by all Christians in the spirit of our Lord's remarks in Matthew 10:42.

We must not think of pollution as affecting merely our own local water supplies. In the early days of legislation, the estuaries were exempt from control. You could dump almost anything there, no questions asked. It was assumed that the oceans would swallow up all the filth they were given. However, even they may be seriously polluted at times, especially when wind and currents return to the shore what had previously been sent to sea. I once lived near an estuary where local authorities on each side were building longer and longer pipelines to discharge raw sewage hopefully into the sea but in fact on to the beaches opposite. At one stage I could not sleep at night for the noise being made by enthusiastic workers on our side laying bigger and better pipes than the opposition!

The oceans can also contain residues from any number of industrial processes on land. A classic case is that of PCBs (polychlorinated biphenyls). These are toxic chemicals long used in electrical equipment as transformers, and though very stable are much more toxic than DDT. When old transformers are dumped near the shore there is every possibility that their contents might be leached out into the oceans. It was reported in 1976 that the waters of the North Atlantic contained 20 parts of PCB per billion. This may not seem much, but it is over twenty times the concentration of DDT and was a considerable cause for alarm because PCBs are so poisonous.

The oceans have always been the destination of unwanted items from shipping, from dead bodies and raw sewage to items of cargo and equipment that don't work. Sometimes this can't be avoided, but often it can. Recently, hundreds of computer monitors were found on a Hong Kong beach, having been apparently dumped at sea, apparently from a ship by people supposed to be recycling them!

However, really big examples of ocean pollution arise when a disaster at sea means spillage of dangerous substances. The first well-documented case of this was the *Torrey Canyon* (in 1967), a giant oil tanker that crashed spilling up to a million tons of oil into the water. Consequently, seabirds and fish died in their thousands. Smaller scale disasters occur round our coasts from time to time and bring home to us the enormous potential for disaster. The carriage of vast quantities of oil and other goods by sea may be a result only of man's greed, but even that sin brings its own retribution. Sadly, it is the animal world, not that of humans, that chiefly suffers. The apparent purity and freshness of the seas we love may conceal a grim reality beneath the waves.

The oceans have indeed been said to be 'the sinks of the world'. We tend to forget that the sink is not bottomless and that there is nowhere else for our unwanted and embarrassing by-products. The oceans are as much our responsibility as the rest of creation.

Polluted air

An island kingdom like Britain is especially subject to mists. Often these come off the seas surrounding us, are due to natural causes and are little more than a nuisance to people on land. Sometimes, however, they become murky palls that we call 'fogs'. Not only is the light blacked out and transport brought to a standstill, but breathing becomes difficult and the fogs can become killers. Almost always they result from material that we throw up into the atmosphere which becomes trapped below a warmer layer of air a few thousand feet above us. London 'pea-soupers' were notorious before World War II, but the worst example since then is the fog of November 1948 which blacked out much of South East England for several weeks. Another one in the early 1950s was nearly as bad and I can clearly remember men with torches walking slowly in front of crawling trolley-buses to guide them through the fog.

FIGURE 4. Smoke from the sea: unlikely pollution (*Mechanics' Magazine*, 1802)

Smoke from the seaside even 200 years ago

A polluted planet   37

Fog is of course no new thing. In 1306, fogs were caused
by burning very poor quality coal. It was so bad that King
Edward I tried to have the culprits executed. Centuries
later Queen Elizabeth I wanted to ban coal altogether, for
it was now certain that this was at least partly responsible.
By Queen Victoria's time the problem was compounded
by all kinds of industry spewing into the atmosphere
unwanted by-products and by coal fires burning in most
homes in a crowded city. Folk who could afford to do
so moved out of London into the country. The smoke-
laden fog was eventually called 'smog', but only after the
disaster in the early 1950s were Clean Air Acts passed to
minimize the problem. It became illegal to burn certain
kinds of fuel, and what industry could throw into the air
was severely limited.

Fogs, however, are only one kind of air pollution. In
the 19th century, there was terrible pollution of the air
through the activities of the chemical industry, driven by
the spiralling demands for soda and acids. The soda was
used then as now for scouring dirty cloth, for making
soap (much more effective as a dirt-remover) and in
the manufacture of glass. Acids were much in demand
for cleaning up metal and (later) for making synthetic
dyes and drugs. One of them, sulphuric acid, was used
in the old method for producing soda. A by-product
was hydrogen chloride, a gas which when let loose in
the atmosphere was a severe health hazard, corroded
railings and other iron structures, and killed crops as
well. A soda producer on Merseyside in the 1830s, an
Irishman called James Muspratt, in those days was often
prosecuted for chemical pollution of the air. He was quite
unrepentant and merely moved his business to another
area, claiming 'all the waters of Ballyshannon could not
condense the acid that I produce'. Later it was realized that
this acid had a corrosive effect on limestone buildings as

well, especially when there was rain. In 1858, a chemist
called R. Angus Smith first wrote of ' acid rain' because
the rain that fell through the atmosphere picked up all
kinds of acid gases and when it reached the ground
was sometimes so strongly acidic that it could dissolve
limestone and corrode iron railings. One casualty was the
Houses of Parliament which, for this reason, have had to
be continuously repaired since about 1870. Another was
St. Paul's Cathedral, where the balustrade lost about 8 mm
per 100 years from 1718 to 1980.

FIGURE 5. Crosfield's plant (*London News*, 1886)

*Industrial pollution from a soap factory: chimneys sprouting from
Crosfield's plant in the 19ᵗʰ century*

Today acid rain is still with us, mainly from coal-burning
power stations (where the coal contains some sulphur),
and also from car emissions, where oxides of nitrogen
are pushed into the atmosphere. Action has been taken in
both these cases; for power stations the issuing vapours

can be 'washed' by currents of water, while new cars are now equipped with catalytic converters. In each case, the damage is reduced, not eliminated. This relief may have come to London and other cities in the West, but it is certainly not the case in other countries. Not long ago, Eastern Europe was a great atmospheric polluter. If the wind was in the wrong direction it was sometimes impossible to see across the street in Cracow, Poland, for instance, though some improvements have now been reported. On one occasion, I was filming in that city but it became quite impossible for the TV cameras to 'see' even across the street!

As the 19th century wore on, chemical emissions continued to poison the atmosphere. There were innumerable cases of further air pollution leading to acid rain, while in certain notorious places in north-east England, especially, the smoke was so bad that (near Billingham) it was reported: 'even the birds cough!'.

It was also grim for the citizens who lived nearby. On Tyneside in the middle of the century a *Guide to Walker* described the place as 'black and overpoweringly hideous', though its residents claimed 'there's no place like Walker'. They were probably right! In nearby Byker, the local postmistress made sure her official visits were only once a week. Often, it was much worse for the workers. Again on Tyneside the alkali workers lost all their teeth because of the acids in the air, and could be recognized by the soft items in their diet they were forced to eat. And all this industry was powered by huge amounts of coal which thus contributed further to the greenhouse effect that we shall deal with later.

The acid came either from sulphur-containing coal or as a by-product of certain chemical works. The chemical poisoning of the atmosphere was driven by one thing: the insistent demands by manufacturers of all kinds for more and more chemicals. There were ways of reducing it, but these methods cost money that some (not all) chemical manufacturers were often reluctant to spend. Eventually, public opinion and a growing sense of responsibility helped to reduce pollution but legislation seemed to be the ultimate answer. Most of the worse cases were in North East or North West England, and so great was the danger they posed that in Britain acts of Parliament had to be passed (the Alkali Acts) to limit severely the amount of acid that could escape into the air. These acts were largely successful and show how pressure of public opinion on government can limit pollution. Today, most industries that make or use chemicals are very environmentally aware. Perhaps the best example is the manufacture of the metal aluminium, used for many things from saucepans to aircraft. Though vast amounts of energy are needed to extract it from its ores, there is little consumption of coal or oil, and much is obtained by using renewable hydroelectric power from Scotland.

Until recently in the West, another major headache has been caused by air containing residues of lead. It was discovered in the 1930s that a substance called tetraethyl lead worked marvels with the cars then being made. It made your engine turn much more smoothly and much faster, so it was added to the petrol (to increase what was called the 'octane number'). The performance-enhancing material was greatly in demand, particularly by drivers of sports cars. By the 1980s, however, it had been shown that the lead spewed out into the air from car exhausts had very damaging effects on health, particularly that of young children living near busy roads. It affected their brains and nervous systems. Accordingly, Britain followed West Germany in drastically reducing lead level in petrol, and this meant a ban on tetraethyl lead. Petrol quality had to be improved and car engines were redesigned.

Unfortunately, this has not happened over all the globe, and the poorest countries still use 'leaded' petrol. Indeed considerable profit is made by firms that manufacture all the ingredients that go into it. As a lethal example of air pollution, it should not be allowed anywhere on Earth.

One final example. In the late 1930s, some substances were discovered that seemed too good to be true. They were the CFCs (chlorofluorocarbons). They were colourless liquids with no unpleasant smell, non-poisonous, were totally non-inflammable and boiled at the right temperatures for a variety of purposes. For two functions they were especially appropriate. One was as refrigerants, and for decades they were the cooling liquids that circulated through our fridges and freezers and air-conditioning systems. If there happened to be a leak, no bad after-effects could be detected and they could be replaced by more of the same. Their other great use was in aerosols; they could be liquefied easily under slight pressures, and as pressure was released they could propel shaving cream to your face or shampoo to your hair, or seductive fragrances to anywhere else. After use the CFCs went up into the atmosphere and were simply forgotten.

At least that was the case until 1985 when a team of Cambridge scientists from the British Antarctic Survey examined the ozone layer over Antarctica and found that it was developing a hole (which has since got bigger) with great danger to human health as the ozone would no longer be able to protect us so effectively from dangerous radiation that could cause skin cancer. This was serious news, but why the change? All too soon it became clear that the chief culprits, doing their own deadly work miles above our heads, were none other than the 'harmless' components of our fridges and sprays, the CFCs. Other substances increase the risk to the ozone but CFCs are mainly the problem. Action in the West followed swiftly and they are now subject to a total ban. Substitutes have had to be found, not always as effective as the originals. Fortunately, there is now evidence from the USA that the ozone hole has stabilized, which suggests that the responses that we have taken were wise. But we need to be constantly vigilant.

Other parts of the chemical industry have had their problems, as in cases of accidental explosion. The worst of these was probably that at Bhopal in India, in 1984, when a tank of poisonous MIC (methyl isocyanate) gas blew up one night and enveloped 200,000 sleeping victims in their homes nearby. There were several thousand fatalities. Nor is the nuclear industry free from blame. The disastrous explosion at Chernobyl near Kiev in early 1986 gave off clouds of radioactive rain that had long term effects as far away as Cumbria and Scotland. The claim that 'it could never happen here' is probably true, but nuclear accidents are just one item in the long catalogue of industry polluting our atmosphere.

Much of this pollution was completely unpredictable, and demonstrates something of the sensitivity and complexity of the part of the environment we all take for granted, the air around us. Taking all into account, it is hard to disagree with one writer who surveyed 'the population explosion, the carcinoma of planless urbanism, the new geological deposits of sewage and garbage', observing that 'no other creature than man ever managed to foul its nest in such short order' (Lynn White, jun.). But that, as the next chapter will show, is not all.

Chapter 4

A ravaged planet

So far we have encountered some of the ways in which humans have managed to foul this Earth by the mountains of litter that we have added to it. As a polluted planet, it may well be unique in our cosmos. There are several important ways in which we have ravaged our planet – sometimes these have been plagues and scourges that we are well rid of. No one will mourn the passing of polio, TB and other diseases even if final pockets of them still remain to be eliminated. What should cause distress is the number of good things that we are destroying.

The problem of waste

Much of what we throw away is not worth keeping. Some of it is harmful, like dangerous poisons, some of it will be destroyed anyway by natural processes, like organic matter that has been infected, and so is simply fit for nothing – a waste of space, as we say. An example of the last kind is the 'salt that has lost its savour', the powder deprived of its essential saltiness, and according to Jesus it is fit only for the rubbish heap (Luke 14:34,5).

Let me give you a more modern example. According to the biblical prophets, nations that are evil or disobedient sometimes become 'wastelands'; Jeremiah and Ezekiel often return to this theme. Coming under the judgement of God was for them like being cast away as a load of rubbish. Fortunately, they were often offered a chance to reform (see Jer. 17:7,8; Ezek. 36:32–36).

For several years, I was privileged to lead parties of sixth form science students on a visit to a sewage works. Why would anyone want to do so, and even enjoy the experience? It was a very special sewage works, just outside Bradford in Yorkshire. Before World War II, and for many years later, most of the world's wool went through Bradford to be processed. It had to be washed, and in this process millions of tons of fat were released from the wool itself. This went down into the sewers, where it sometimes tended to block them up. Then someone came up with the brilliant idea of actually filtering off this fat and selling it. They had to coagulate the fat by adding acid to the sewage and had a plant by the works for making sulphuric acid. The process was so successful that not only fats but also lanolin was taken out, and the products were sold for such diverse purposes as axle-grease for railway wagons and face creams. It made such a 'fat' income (excuse the pun) that for years the Esholt sewage works was the only one in the world to operate at a profit! And at the end of the purification, the water was stored in a lake from which visitors were invited to take a drink. Most of the students were rather reluctant to do so! But the advantage was clear, not only for the council bills but also for the environment. Noxious waste had been effectively removed, and, in this case, some unexpected advantages had followed.

The real problem arises when obviously *good* things are simply thrown away – that is waste in its true sense. And that is what human beings do in abundance. It is what the Prodigal Son did while blowing his inheritance in a foreign country (Luke 15:13), and is so obviously wrong that the Bible almost takes this understanding for granted. But not quite. Judas complained 'to what purpose is this waste?' A woman had emptied probably several litres of an expensive perfumery oil over Jesus, soon before his death. Judas failed to understand that her devotion to Christ put all other priorities in the shade. In other circumstances, his cry would have been justified. More to the point, perhaps, is the instruction given by Jesus to his friends after the incredible feeding of over 5,000 people in the desert. At the end of the meal, they were systematically to 'Gather the pieces that are left over. Let nothing be wasted' (John 6:12). If miraculous bread and fish is not to be wasted that is surely true of the food that comes to us by ordinary means. Yet the fact is that we live in what is aptly called 'a throwaway society'.

I was once in a restaurant in the USA and ordered a steak, expecting a maximum of about 8 ounces. When it turned out to be over twice that quantity, and I gently complained, I was firmly told by the waiter, 'Eat all you can and the rest will be thrown away – we always do that!' The same thing happened when a pizza for one had a diameter of about 14 inches. I ought to have known.

In the UK, the situation is not quite so bad, but we are in no position to throw stones at the USA. A recent report (2007) revealed that Britons throw away 30 per cent of their good food. Sometimes this is because the sell-by date is passed, sometimes because food at the back of the fridge is forgotten, sometimes because children will not eat what is given to them, but often it is simply because of over-buying. The ridiculous habit of supermarkets offering 'Buy one, get one free' is partly to blame, though they pass the blame on to the gullibility of customers facing an apparent bargain. That is only an excuse. They could just as easily offer single items at half the price of their current offer – it would be much easier for small families and avoid huge national wastage. As things are, this dubious practice relies on the simple fact of our over-buying. The unwanted food ends up in landfill sites where (apart from attracting vermin) it slowly decomposes and gives off methane. This causes another set of problems, as we shall see.

When we consider how many people in the world are starving, over-production in some places can lead to waste on a scale that we can't defend. Sometimes what is left is thrown to tame or wild animals, which is better than burying it, but reminiscent of Jesus' injunction to his disciples not to cast their pearls (valuable things) before swine (Matt. 7:6).

There are still people around old enough to have been children during World War II. They will recall – doubtless with a shudder – how many families managed to survive food rationing and other deprivations by never throwing edible food away and always finding a way to use it. With post-war plenty and a booming economy, Britons no longer take that view. As we shall see, there are potent reasons for still doing so, but meanwhile we can continue to recognize that over-production and prodigal wastage of good things is another way in which we have all ravaged this planet.

Dead as a dodo

That famous bird the dodo no longer exists. Unable to fly, it was a sitting target for human hunters and was hunted to extinction. Whether the planet is a poorer place without the dodo we cannot judge. There are plenty of other beasts that will soon join it as just a memory. When did you last see a butterfly in your garden, or even a sparrow? Is the dawn chorus of birds less clear than it used to be? If you live in the country you will be even more aware of the disappearance of once-familiar birds and animals. Many of them are still there, but in smaller numbers; they are on the way to extinction even if some have quite a long way to go.

There are lots of reasons for these changes, and not all of them are man-made. Yet there are two potent cases for which we as a race are responsible. One, as Carson pointed out, is the use of insecticides and other pest-controllers. Rather than calling for a total ban, however, we now know that we must be discriminating and use them in much smaller quantities and much more carefully. Where GM crops are grown, selective weed killers are often used to destroy every plant except the one desired as a crop. Their effect on wildlife can be devastating.

The other big cause is destruction of habitats. The hedges in which many creatures once lived have been swept away by farmers anxious to use for crop production every square metre of land. This not only threatens nesting birds but also the smaller creatures and fruits on which they live. This is another example of the evils of over-production. Something very like this is explicitly condemned by the Bible. When the Israelites were reaping their crops they were forbidden to harvest to the very edges of the field, but told to leave the edges. One consequence would be that the poor could glean some corn, etc. for themselves (see Lev. 19:9).

Another example was that land could have some kind of 'rest'. This need was more dramatically recognized by the institution of the Jubilee system, where, once in every 50 years, the ground should be left un-tilled and people were to treat each other specially well. What is more, something similar happened more frequently than that: 'For six years sow your fields, and for six years prune your vineyards and gather their crops. But in the seventh year the land is to have a sabbath of rest, a sabbath to the LORD.

Do not sow your fields or prune your vineyards' (Lev. 25:3,4). Even the land was worthy of respect and rest. How far the Israelites actually obeyed these commandments we do not know. What is certain is that we, in the modern West, have ignored them at our peril, and to the great devastation of our ravaged planet.

This of course is also true of our oceans. Over-fishing off the North Sea has hurt the stocks of fish and the livelihoods of fishermen. It is not they who are to blame but rather those whose greed demands more and more and are somehow able to pay for it.

There is a third kind of danger facing our wildlife, in addition to pesticides and over-farming. That is hunting by human beings. Whether hunting is always undesirable is still a matter of fierce debate. There are often far worse fates for any animal, some natural (like lying injured and helpless) or inflicted by us (like intensive farming) and after all fishing is only another name for hunting in the waters. However, fox-hunting with dogs is now banned in the UK and there is some kind of legal protection for other animals under threat, such as badgers. Many birds are now protected species as are their eggs and nests.

Recent studies have shown that hunting to extermination is no new thing; what we think of as our contemporary problem has in fact been with us for ages. Human nature has hardly changed. In our islands, the hunting of birds and animals has been pursued for centuries, for a variety of reasons, all of which reflect the self-centredness of humans. As a result, whole species have disappeared completely, or else been driven to a precarious survival in remote areas. They include the polecat, pine marten, wild cat, and countless kinds of birds.

The most obvious reason for hunting has always been *to obtain food*. Since Mesolithic times, the wild boar has been hunted for its meat, though more recently to avoid cross-breeding with the common pig. Many place names attest to its presence, as in Wild Boar Fell in Cumbria (allegedly where the last of the species was shot). Other parts of Britain claim this dubious honour, such as the Forest of Dean. Recent attempts have been made to reintroduce it to the wild.

Slaughter was often *a matter of human survival*, and as such has some justification. Thus the bear seems to have been exterminated in Britain well before the Norman Conquest, perhaps about 700 AD. Much less dangerous, but still a threat to young children, was the wolf which managed to survive another thousand years. Smaller creatures that posed a threat to human health included rats and mice. These are still being pursued as 'vermin'. How that term is defined depends on social conditions, to say nothing of scientific knowledge. Few suspects were given the benefit of the doubt in earlier centuries. By Tudor times, 'Vermin Acts' were introduced (e.g. in 1525) giving churchwardens the power to reward people who successfully exterminated the named animals or birds. Extensive 'control' of wildlife seems to have begun in the 17th century. It was widely extended by the invention of steel traps and the use of guns in the next century, and by new methods of poisoning thereafter.

Very soon creatures were hunted because of their perceived threat to property. This was true of birds of prey, like eagles, that were known to attack small sheep and lambs. When in Scotland sheep farmers replaced tenant farmers after the Highland Clearances, persecution of such birds reached new levels. Some birds were treated ambiguously. The red kites were actually given protection orders in cities, as they were believed to act as scavengers of urban garbage. However, in the countryside they were hated and virtually eliminated by the 19th century. A very few survivors in remote parts of Central Wales, with much human help, became the nucleus of a small return of the birds this century.

With far less justification, hunting was also pursued for personal adornment. Long after bear-skins ceased to be available, beavers were hunted for their fur until they too became extinct in about the 17th century. Moles have been sought for the same reason, one good Victorian waistcoat requiring skins from a hundred animals. Now they are still being persecuted for the damage they inflict on cultivated lands. At present they seem likely to survive. The most barbarous case within the last 150 years is probably that of the kittiwakes in East Yorkshire. They were caught, deprived of their wings and then (still alive) cast into the sea to drown. The wings were used to adorn the hats of Victorian women, each of whom wore 'a murderer's brand upon her head', as one critic put it.

Even less defensible is the ravaging of our Earth for sheer entertainment alone. Of course, there was heady pleasure for the companions of John Peel, the famous huntsman in Cumbria, as they paraded before the hunt or as the pursuit drew to a close. Presumably the same applies to modern hunting on the grouse-moors of the north. Cruelty for its own sake is much more questionable, but such undoubtedly occurred in the barbarous practice of cockfighting, not banned till 1840. In Kendal, a street called Beast Banks still testifies to the inhuman practice of baiting animals before they were killed for meat. It was permitted until 1791, by which time the amount of animal suffering must have been immense. The red squirrel is now subject to protection orders, but an old gamekeeper from Bedfordshire was reported as saying he killed squirrels, not because they did evident harm, rather 'but what good do they do?' This is killing for its own sake, and therefore for pleasure alone.

Fortunately, the fearsome elimination of native species did not go unchallenged. By the early 18th century there had been a new rise in natural awareness, with nature seen not as a menace, but as something to be studied and even cherished. Christian writers like John Ray doubtless played an important part here, but so did a rising awareness of science itself. Thus by the 18th century, naturalistic writing was encountered in literature as Gray's *Seasons* or Gilbert White's *Natural History of Selborne* of 1789. In art, the work of Constable and especially the horse paintings by Stubbs showed a new realism and will have made nature seem somehow not so threatening. But anything like a conservation movement was a long way off in Britain.

Overseas, the planet continued to be ravaged. Whales have long been hunted, ostensibly for their meat and blubber. As a result their numbers in the seas have drastically fallen. This is especially true in the waters around Japan and northern Canada and various national agreements are in place to curtail whale-hunting. They are still in peril from pirate-hunters and governments who renege on their agreements.

Species of the Asian tiger are on the verge of extinction. One has been a victim of the hunt for the supposed healing powers of parts of its body, being much prized by the devotees of Chinese medicine. The Asiatic lion is now down to about 300 animals, in one area of India. The orang-utan population of Borneo has been nearly halved in the last 10 years, much of it due to poachers, and around 1,000 animals are lost each year. Partly this reflects a demand for baby animals as pets, involving killing the mother to capture them. About three of these events take place every day.

A more familiar species is in great danger within the Arctic. The polar bear is threatened chiefly by diminishing numbers of fish to eat (the stocks are only likely to last another 15 years) and rapid melting of the ice due to global warming. As a species, it is unlikely to survive beyond this century.

Such tales of doom and gloom could be endlessly repeated. Some figures recently available confirm our pessimism. Since the year 1600 it is believed that at least 484 species of animals and 654 species of plants have disappeared for ever. In our lifetimes, the rates of extinction have been estimated to be over 1,000 times faster than before, and now about three species are likely to have been eliminated every day. We are losing what has been called 'biodiversity'. Some will be inevitably reduced if we aim for a development of our planet that is sustainable, but the present rate of loss is quite unacceptable to those who believe that the sheer variety of God's creation is there for a purpose and adds to his praise. Yet there are still people who deny that planet Earth has been at all damaged by human activity. They regard as busybodies anyone who draws concerned attention to our ravaged planet. Who is right? How far should we recognize the intrinsic worth of all creatures? The book of Job suggests that *all* are of interest to God, timid ones, small ones as well as those of terrifying behaviour.

'Hurt not the trees'

There is one special part of our environment whose loss would cause untold damage to all our lives in the future. That is the world of trees. One of the more intriguing commands given by the angel in the book of Revelation was this: 'Hurt not the earth, neither the sea, nor the trees' (Rev. 7:3, AV). What is interesting is that in this general command to spare our world from total destruction is the special mention of 'trees'. Why were they singled out?

Quite possibly this re-emphasizes a notion that is present elsewhere in Scripture, the importance of trees. Their destruction is widely condemned, even if they belonged to the Israelites' enemies (Deut. 20:19) and is deeply mourned when it happens to them (e.g. Joel 1:12,19). The Babylonian King Nebuchadnezzar is taken to task by his Maker for destruction of the magnificent cedars north of Israel: 'You have cut down the forests of Lebanon; now you will be cut down' (Hab. 2:17, GNB). 'Even the pine trees and the cedars of Lebanon exult over you and say, "Now that you have been laid low, no woodsman comes to cut us down"' (Isa. 14:8). Often the trees were prized because of their obvious value to people as bearers of fruit. Thanks to modern science, we are now much more aware of how important trees are. In short, it is because they will absorb carbon dioxide from the air, and replace it with oxygen. That is the reverse of what mammals do, so trees help to maintain the 'cycle' of natural operations whereby our atmosphere has neither too much nor too little of its main components. Trees are vital to animal life on earth.

All over Britain we find traces of forests that once covered many square miles. Sometimes they have been recently taken over for building land. More often they were simply over-exploited for their products. Take the Weald that once covered vast areas of Sussex and Kent. For centuries, it has been used to provide trees for the Royal Navy, in the days when ships were chiefly made of wood. For a long time, trees were cut down in their millions and burned to make charcoal. This was used for extracting metals from their ores and thus in the manufacture of iron. Later it was employed in huge quantities as one of the three ingredients of gunpowder. By the Napoleonic Wars, the government simply couldn't get enough of it. So today we find attractive relics of once great forests in places like Ashdown Forest and in villages like Abinger Hammer whose 'hammer-ponds' were sites of water-powered machinery for flattening the newly obtained iron.

Our loss in Britain is far smaller and less serious than that in tropical countries. In the early 1990s, the rainforests of the world were estimated to cover nine million square kilometres. Now they are disappearing at the rate of about 110,000 square kilometres every year. That is about 1 per cent each year. This is largely because of 'logging' where trees are felled for their timber or to make wooden pulp for cheap furniture.

The most important rainforest is that in the Amazon Basin in South America. The Brazilian government has taken stern steps to preserve it, but illegal logging is still responsible for great losses. In Borneo, the famous Sumatran Forest has all but disappeared and in 20 years has lost an area eight times that of Wales. Other forests in that area are rapidly shrinking and are predicted to disappear by 2020.

There are several reasons why loss of the rainforests should alarm us all. In fact, they cover only 7 per cent of the earth's surface, but they are said to harbour 60 per cent of the world's species. It has been argued that 10,000 species have been lost through rainforest destruction. To take only one example, the loss of forest in Borneo is a major cause of the threat to orang-utans. That alone should sting us into action. Yet there is an even more powerful reason in the effect on the carbon cycle.

Of course, the 'carbon cycle' is much more complicated than I previously summarized, but it is clear that wide-spread destruction of trees will lead to a surplus of carbon dioxide in the air. Its presence will lead to consequences that are so serious that much of the other damage to our planet is small in comparison. These are changes in our climate that are currently the most serious threat to planet

Earth. They demand a chapter of their own. But before that, one other, and very obvious, feature of our ravaged planet needs to be mentioned.

Standing room only

This is the question of overpopulation. While some species are threatened and then eliminated, there is one that seems to be quite secure: that is *homo sapiens*, the human race. In apparent obedience to Genesis 1:28, we continue to 'multiply' and replenish the Earth. More will be said about this verse later, but meanwhile we have to concede that much of the extinctions already mentioned must be laid at the door of an expanding world population of men and women.

In Britain, it's all too obvious now. Our transport systems are so overcrowded that recently one pressure group introduced a model sardine ('Mr Sardine Man') into a commuter train to make the point about our railways, while driving can be a daytime nightmare for those who have to traverse the M25, otherwise known as 'Britain's linear car park'. Similar experiences are to be had at supermarket stores at peak times, in schools with classes that are far too big, and above all at our airports. Of course, it did not suddenly happen; Gustav Doré was fond of illustrating Victorian London, where, as his picture shows (see Figure 6) things were far from easy, but other cities were getting nearly as crowded and 100 years later we all now experience it. However, there are ways of escaping congestion on the roads – by travelling at night or taking holidays in remote places in England, Scotland, Wales or Ireland. Nor must we assume that British experience is typical – it is far worse in places in the East or Latin America, and far better in New Zealand (for instance) where a land mass about the size of Britain

FIGURE 6. Drawing by Gustav Doré

Crowded London in the 19ᵗʰ century

has to support only 15 per cent of our population. In the British case, increase in population is not so much due to expanding birth rates (on the whole they are decreasing) but rather the large numbers of immigrants, legal or otherwise, who end up in our country.

What is really worrying is the overall global trend. Thus in 1977 the world population was over 4.25 billion and increasing by 77 million per year (UN Sources). Now, around 30 years later it is about 6.5 billion. Since 1950 the global population has doubled! There are all sorts of reasons that prompt families to expand in the Third World, just as there are others which encourage other families to keep to smaller numbers and fewer mouths to feed. Few are remotely aware of the global issues involved. The scientific facts, however, are often in short supply, and good service is being done by radio broadcasts that include contraceptive advice as well as the deeper issues, scientific and spiritual, at stake.

Clearly, this trend cannot be allowed to continue as resources of land, food water and fuel are not limitless. Much increase is due to modern medicine, because of which more babies survive into adulthood, and thereafter people are better equipped to deal with the diseases and accidents that affect us all our lives. So what are the solutions?

No one in their right mind would propose to reduce the level of medical care available; indeed it needs to be greatly increased in poorer parts of the world. Nor can there be any justification for forcibly reducing the expected lifespan of older individuals or of unwanted babies (of either sex). Both fly in the face of clear biblical injunctions to care for the weak and not to kill – child-murder, for example, was common in the centuries before Christ and is roundly condemned throughout the Old Testament.

The only way forward must therefore be in the limiting of the global birth rate. Contraceptive advice, however well-meant, encounters two major hurdles. One branch of the Christian church (the Roman Catholics) have consistently opposed it as 'against nature' and contrary to God's will. If followed this would also mean a disproportionate increase in one section of the population, the followers of that faith. It so happens that much evidence has suggested that in many parts of the world devout Roman Catholics pay little heed to this prohibition. Also, opponents of contraception may also advise limitation of families by straightforward abstinence. Each must follow his or her conscience.

The other opposition comes from another Christian source. Some missionary radio stations that have ventured to provide advice on contraception have been rebuffed by the accusation that this is merely an excuse for licentious living. The suggestion is made that 'no sex before marriage' should have been commended instead. While such advice is good, it rather misses the point that contraception may be commended *within* the married state, but unfortunately it has attracted this unwelcome association with promiscuous living. There can be little hope for the planet if its population increases to breaking point. The only possibility is that we colonize another planet somewhere in the universe. But this is easier said than done.

Chapter 5

The big one: climate change

The famous English writer Dr. Johnson once said 'when two Englishmen meet, their first talk is of the weather'. Possibly, this is what makes us specially English, perhaps our most endearing national characteristic. In America, however, Mark Twain once noted that for New England the climate was so varied that within 24 hours 'I have counted 136 different kinds of weather'. Neither he nor Johnson could have been aware of something much more interesting, the fact that these climates were changing. We now live in a state of *climate change.*

Everyone's talking about it: newspapers, TV, radio, anybody who notices how warm it is outside, people planning their holidays, farmers, gardeners and many more. Even politicians have jumped on the bandwagon, with one political party after another claiming to be more 'green' than the others. In fact, climate change has become the big 'green' issue of today. However, as we've already seen, there are lots of other things that should worry us nearly as much. Once upon a time, the 'greenest' of all the protest groups were those who opposed every kind of artificial insecticides. Times have changed and so have fashions. But the evidence available today does suggest that changes in our climate could affect us all to such an extent that pollution of various kinds would be something that goes almost unnoticed.

The argument is really very simple: the Earth is experiencing something called 'global warming', is getting hotter by the year and this will have all sorts of unpleasant consequences. What is more, we human beings are partly responsible. If so, we should do what we can to put things right. That is the generally received view, but it can get brushed aside by two other reactions. One is to pretend it won't happen, or at least to *leave it well alone*. Recently, I was in our local chemist's shop on a hot spring day. After I had been given my purchases, the conversation went something like this as I was about to leave.

> ME: 'Thank you very much.'
>
> FIRST SHOP ASSISTANT: 'Pleasure. It's a warm day, isn't it?'
>
> ME: 'It certainly is.'
>
> FIRST SHOP ASSISTANT: 'They say it's all warming up.'
>
> ME: 'You mean "climate change"?'
>
> FIRST SHOP ASSISTANT: 'I suppose I do …'
>
> ME: 'It's certainly happening …'
>
> SECOND SHOP ASSISTANT: 'Please don't talk about that. I never want to hear it again and I always stop my ears when it's mentioned. Too horrible!'

That young lady was only about 18 and yet was all too willing to ignore anything that might affect the long years in front of her. Yet I'm sure she spoke for many.

The other approach is *robust denial*. This was taken recently in a TV programme 'The Great Global Warming Swindle' in which a small group of scientists, and some well-known politicians who knew little about science, took on the view of the scientific establishment and pronounced it mistaken. Their target was the International Panel on Climate Change, a group appointed by most world governments with over 200 delegates from about 100 countries. They had complete freedom to investigate as they wished and the Committee's fourth Assessment Report was published in February 2007. It was in line with a statement to the G8 Summit of 2005 from the Academies of Science of the 11 largest countries of the world, those of the G8 nations and also India, Brazil and China.

It does not need a Christian to point out that scientists – like other mortals – can easily make mistakes. We are fallible beings. But when there is such a complete agreement among the leaders of world science, with very few real scientists dissenting, the world has a right to take them seriously. They have been defended by Sir John Houghton, an evangelical Christian who was Chairman of the Working Party that initially presented the science. He considers the opposition as 'a mixture of truth, half-truth and falsehood'. That is our position here. So what does science really say? Let's begin at the beginning.

The strange story of carbon

Imagine a very simple experiment. Take two saucers and put a bit of charcoal – the kind used in barbecues – on one of them. If we now put this charcoal in a flame it will burn brightly and leave almost nothing behind. That is exactly what we should expect.

Now place on the second saucer a bright diamond, in someone's ring, for instance. If you were now to burn this (that's why I suggest you 'imagine' the experiment!) you would find the diamond also disappeared and burned away. This very experiment was actually once performed by an English chemist called Sir Humphry Davy while visiting Florence in 1814 (Florence was not the lady who gave him the ring, but the city in Italy!). What this shows is that diamond and charcoal are essentially the same thing.

We call it carbon, and diamond is actually the purest form of it. Diamond is an enduring substance (unless you set fire to it) and one reason is its hardness (the hardest thing on Earth). Diamond is simply an assembly of carbon atoms, each of which is bound to another four; and the 'bonds' that hold it together are extremely strong.

The carbon-to-carbon bond is quite exceptional. Of all the natural 92 elements of chemistry, carbon is *the only one that can go on joining to other atoms of itself.* This makes for three dimensional assemblies like diamond, rings of carbon atoms present in charcoal and graphite, but above all chains of almost any length. So the number of possible compounds carbon can form is huge. These variations – with other atoms added as well – include basic units of proteins, carbohydrates, fats, steroids and millions of other molecules. Together, they make it possible for life to exist. Very few if any of our neighbouring planets in space have this incredible element. From a human being to a tiny virus, all living things are made of carbon. When eventually living creatures die, they are returned to the dust, so also does their carbon. If they are trees they may end up as coal, but if they are small sea creatures they may form petroleum. Other bodies may yield methane or carbon dioxide.

All this may seem miles away from climate change, but it isn't really. There is an even stranger tale to tell. The reason why Davy was so sure that diamond and charcoal were basically the same element is that they both formed the same thing when they were burned. It is an invisible gas called carbon dioxide, or CO_2 as it is often called. This is the gas that we breathe out every few seconds of our life. It is formed from the oxygen in the air as we inhale, and the resultant process, like combustion, gives us the energy we need. The same is true of most animals but not plants. Fish depend on the oxygen dissolved in the waters surrounding them, but still breathe out CO_2.

Even more remarkable is the other side of the picture. Vegetables, and especially trees, will take up CO_2 from the air under the influence of sunlight, and this is how they grow. No wonder Scripture so emphasizes the value of trees! In behaving in this way, trees and other plants release oxygen into the atmosphere, thus providing a

FIGURE 7. Diamond

A partial model of a giant diamond molecule. The black balls stand for carbon atoms

marvellous balancing act. As a result, the concentration of CO_2 is normally pretty constant, a mere 280 ppm (parts per million). Scientists call these processes the 'carbon cycle' and life on Earth depends on them. It takes quite a lot of faith to believe this all happened by accident, but it is just another example of God's wonderful provision. In a world that contained no carbon, diamonds wouldn't exist and all life would be totally impossible.

The strange fact about today is that now the CO_2 levels in the air are a little higher than has been the case for ages and are about 375 ppm. They seem to be creeping up. The differences aren't huge but they could be quite enough

FIGURE 8. Some simple carbon compounds

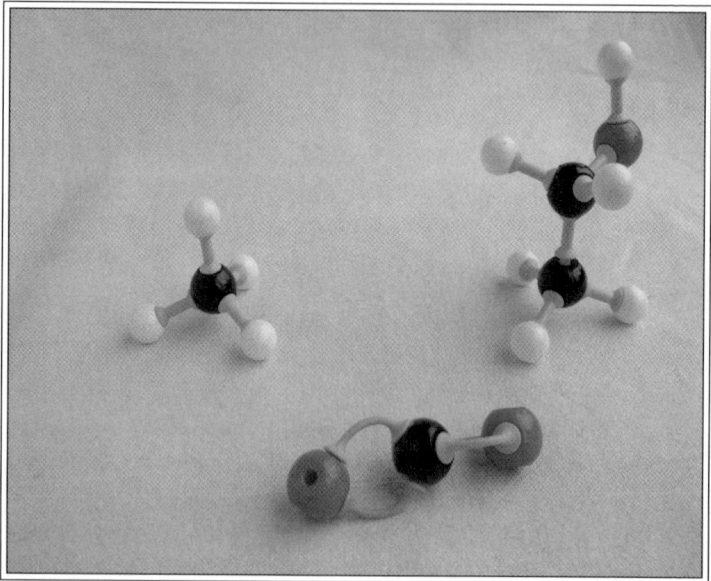

Some simple carbon-containing molecules. From left to right they are methane, carbon dioxide and alcohol (or ethanol)

to damage our whole environment. We need to ask why CO_2 levels are rising.

Globes and greenhouses

If you have a greenhouse you will know that on warm summer days it may get too hot inside even for the sensitive plants you are trying to grow. So you open a few windows, perhaps the door, and get the temperature down to the right level. It's much the same for the globe we inhabit.

For hundreds, probably millions, of years our Earth had been relentlessly bombarded with everything the sun can throw at it. Solar rays include heat, together with all kinds of waves and particles we would rather not have. We also have an atmosphere that can let most of the sun's rays through, though the ozone layer filters off the harmful 'hard' ultraviolet rays. One thing[1] that prevents us from frying alive is that the Earth turns on its axis every 24 hours, so we have mercifully cooler nights. Other planets aren't so fortunate. The one nearest the sun, Mercury, always faces the sun so on that side it is so hot that even lead would melt, while on the other side it is so cold that even gases familiar to us would turn solid. Our nearest neighbour, Venus, does rotate but it has no atmosphere like ours and, with a very high temperature, would not support life.

---

[1] There is actually a second provision that helps us in the temperate zones, and that is that Earth's rotating axis is not at right angles to the plane of our path around the sun, so only the tropics get the worst of the sun's radiation. And everyone on Earth benefits from a third arrangement which is that our orbit round the sun does not have the sun at its centre, so every 365 days we have both longer and shorter seasons: summer and winter. This, God promised, will continue to the end of time (see Gen. 8:22).

One consequence of our receiving all that heat from the sun is that we manage to keep (mostly!) comfortably warm, though the Earth also gets some heat from naturally radioactive minerals in its interior. We know that about 30 per cent of the sun's radiation is reflected back at it, mainly by clouds, but there is one snag. The carbon dioxide in our air helps to absorb natural radiation *from* the Earth, so we get warmer than would otherwise be the case. In its absence, the expected average temperature would be around $-18°C$, but in fact the average is about $+15°C$. In other words, CO_2 acts just like the glass in our greenhouse. And carbon dioxide is said to exert a 'greenhouse effect'.

Other 'greenhouse gases' have the same effect, such as methane from landfills, water vapour and all the artificial substances like CFCs that we once threw into the air. Now CFCs are banned because of their effects on the ozone layer. One chemical used in making less ozone-unfriendly chemicals is trifluoromethane. If let loose in the air it would have a greenhouse effect 11,700 times that of CO_2! Fortunately, it can be easily removed by manufacturers. But CO_2 is the one that has been most studied and there is no doubt that in the past, higher amounts have meant higher temperatures.

We know quite a lot about past climates. Part of our information comes from literature and art (e.g. paintings of the frozen Thames in the great freezes of the 17th century), from annual tree-rings in fallen tree branches or trunks (where a wide space between rings means a warmer summer) and above all from the cores taken out of the ice in the polar regions. These cores are cross-sections of the ice at that place for probably several thousands of years. Like tree trunks, they can tell us what the temperatures were like, and as the air is trapped as bubbles in the ice, they can give a correlation between temperature and CO_2 levels in that air. It is astonishingly close. There is no longer any real room for doubt that carbon dioxide is related to the greenhouse effect on our globe.

It should be readily admitted that CO_2 is not the only cause for global warming. Natural cycles of the weather exist and they should not be forgotten. An example is that special explosions on the face of the sun, sunspots, may also increase our temperatures. Such solar activity has now been monitored for several hundred years and (for instance) has been shown to be very small during the mini-Ice Age of the 16th to the 19th centuries. Nevertheless, these cycles are only part of the story, and carbon dioxide remains a main culprit.

But what does global warming do and does it matter?

Global warming: good or bad?

First the facts. The prestigious American organization NASA has recorded a rise in global temperature of 0.6°C in the last 30 or so years. Not much, perhaps, but recall that 2005 had the hottest summer on record. The IPCC predicts that by the end of the century the average temperature will rise by amounts varying from 1.4°C to 3.9°C. Very recently (Nov. 2007) the IPCC has suggested that a rise of only 2.5°C would threaten nearly a third of animal and bird species, while a rise of 4°C would cause 'significant extinctions'.

Many Britons quite like the idea of global warming. The prospect of relatively mild winters, glorious springs and hot summers is rather attractive. It brings back childhood memories of basking on British beaches, and many relish the thought. After all, if we can't or won't travel overseas for holidays as much as once we did, all that is left might be the likes of Blackpool, Bournemouth or the fabled Cornish Riviera. So let's make the most of it, they say.

And why not? The problem, however, is that Britons on holiday are only a tiny proportion of the world's population, and the overall effects of global warming for the rest of our neighbours on this planet are anything but pleasant. Those who would be worse affected are those who can ill afford to avoid it: the world's poor. If we are to help them as well as ourselves, we must try to paint a realistic picture, even at the risk of sounding like the prophets of doom. Christians will be familiar with this process, for before anyone comes to Christ he/she must be aware of their need.

So what happens if global warming continues to occur?

1. Unpredictability

Here we are entering unknown territory. Though some things may be safely predicted, there are others about which we know all too little. Summer and winter will continue, but they will have surprises for us. We know this because the warming of the last 20 or 30 years has already brought its own crop of shocks. There are plenty of tales of the unexpected.

Here is the experience of Maurice Onyango, a Christian Aid Emergency Programme Officer working in Kenya (as reported in the *Developments* magazine of DFID):

> Talk to the farmers, they will tell you that previously they could predict the seasons, quite accurately. They knew when to plant, when to prepare the seeds, but it is no longer the case. Even the meteorological department can't always predict the weather.

Farmers the world over are going to be in this predicament. The problem is that the weather is a complex business, resulting mainly from changing wind patterns and these are bound to alter as the climate changes. Tiny changes in one area can give spectacular effects miles away. To give a simple example from the UK, some years ago the course of the River Kent was slightly altered as it flowed into the sea at Morecambe Bay. No one knows exactly what that alteration was. The result was a silting up of the foreshore of Grange-over-Sands on the north bank of the estuary, and its takeover by acres of useless and unsightly Spartina grass. On that side of the water, no one did anything about it for some time and now the problem is too big to solve. The whole ecology of the system has changed.

On a far bigger scale is the possibility that climate change might induce a change in the direction of the Gulf Stream current in the eastern Atlantic that warms our north-eastern shores. If the Gulf Stream were to be diverted, Scotland would become an arctic wilderness and the economy of Britain would be altered beyond recognition. The whole point is that no one knows, and unpredictability reigns.

Unpredictability arises especially when we consider what some have called 'natural disasters', just because we had no rational explanation for them. The insurance companies once used to call them 'acts of God', though their use of 'God' as an explanation of anything they could not account for otherwise was deplorable. Disasters range from tsunamis to floods to earthquakes. The interesting thing is that their number has trebled in the last 30 years; populations affected have risen from 74 million to 245 million per annum. Most of these unpredictable disasters now seem to have been weather-related; though that obviously excludes earthquakes and volcanoes. In view of the influence of climate change on the weather, we must lay many of these distressing events at its door. And if it can be shown that humanity has a part to play in global warming, 'acts of God' could well become 'acts of humanity' instead. But that's another story.

There are other things that we can predict with much greater certainty. Here is one of them.

2. Drought

The drying effects of a hotter atmosphere are obvious. Among other things there will arise an acute shortage of drinking water. This, we have already seen, is a terrible fate for those who currently suffer shortages of pure water. Given more drought conditions, the least important annoyance is the imposition in the UK of hosepipe bans. Millions in the undeveloped world will perish from thirst or from drinking polluted water. It is reckoned that, if present trends continue, by the end of this century three billion people will have perished from water shortages in the Middle East alone. We cannot sit idly by, knowing this is certainly going to happen if global warming increases.

There is another consequence, too – the process known as desertification, in which once fertile land becomes inhospitable and useless because it turns into deserts. Deserts already cover nearly one-quarter of the Earth's land-surface. Desertification is increasing rapidly. It will particularly affect sub-Saharan Africa where the ground will not become a desert but will be much less fertile than it used to be and the growing year will be appreciably shortened. The effect on farmers can be imagined.

Nor is the Two-Thirds World the only part of our Earth to be affected. The year 2003 saw a heatwave and drought that led to losses of $124 million in the USA. The area of the Earth hit by serious drought has doubled since 1970.

3. Rising waters

When global warming takes over, the ice caps in the Polar regions begin to melt. This process has happened in earlier ages, and at one time Greenland did not have 'icy mountains' and worldwide ice was much less. But for centuries, perhaps millennia, the ice has returned, some of it melting in high summer with icebergs breaking off and then drifting on the oceans for months (as voyagers in the *Titanic* knew to their cost). Now there is clear evidence that the ice is beginning to melt again on a larger scale than anything we have ever known. Pictures have been taken in 2002 of a giant iceberg appearing in the Antarctic. This block of ice was 200 metres thick and had an area of 3,250 square kilometres. Since most of each iceberg is below the ocean surface, and since all of it will eventually melt, this has one effect: sea water levels will rise all over the globe.

In Britain we are aware of the power of the seas whenever we visit the coast and hear waves lashing the shore. When this is accompanied by higher sea levels, their force is much greater. On the English east coast this is often obvious. In Scarborough, for example, several houses or hotels near the cliff face have had to be evacuated as the crumbling soil below is pounded by the sea. Further south, the medieval village of Dunwich has disappeared beneath the waves, church, houses, pub and all. That happened long ago (the cliffs are especially soft just there) but it shows what can occur if land is exposed to the force of the sea.

Unfortunately, a great deal of inhabited land is much lower than the cliffs of Dunwich. Many parts of the African coast and countries like Bangladesh support millions of people even though the land may be only a metre or so above present sea levels. Strangely, part of the Earth will suffer from acute water shortages, while another part will be flooded out of existence.

Inland, snows are beginning to disappear from some mountain tops. This is painfully obvious to the skiing fraternity in the Cairngorms, for instance. Much more serious is the melting of snow caps on mountains as far away as Africa, where torrents of water flowing down them can cause serious, if local, problems of flooding.

4. Health problems

It is hardly surprising if climate change causes disease. A higher temperature is threatening to the old and very young. Thus the heatwave of 2003 caused 30,000 deaths in Europe, with a death rate up by 54 per cent for those over 45. One effect of global warming will be an increase of ozone concentrations at ground levels. As opposed to the ozone layer far above our heads ozone gas at levels where we breathe is a thoroughly bad thing. Rather than attracting us to the bracing beaches of the east coast (as was misleadingly advertized before the last world war), increased ozone amounts should fill us with concern. Here at ground level, ozone is formed by the sun acting on car exhausts, and in the UK 2,500 people died from it in 2003. At higher temperatures, ozone levels will increase, and with them the risks to health.

In less temperate zones, malaria, polio, etc. are all increased by heat. In Africa one child dies every second from malaria, and in sub-Saharan Africa, by the end of this century, 182 million people could die of diseases directly attributable to climate change.

Who's to blame?

Up to about 1800, the evidence from ice-cores shows that the temperatures and CO_2 contents of the atmosphere have been remarkably constant. Then, around that year, temperatures slowly started to increase. No one was seriously bothered. Then in the 1980s, attention was focused and alarm bells started to ring. For, from about 1865, the rise in temperature became much faster, and at the end of the 19th century it had steepened sharply.

By our own day, it is rising so rapidly that you really need a graph to appreciate it. There have been numerous attempts to predict the future trends. Although the final forecasts differ from each other a little, according to the assumptions of their calculators, they all agree that by the end of this century the globe we inhabit will be unacceptably hot.

FIGURE 9. Temperature graph (J. Houghton and IPCC, Prince Philip Lecture)

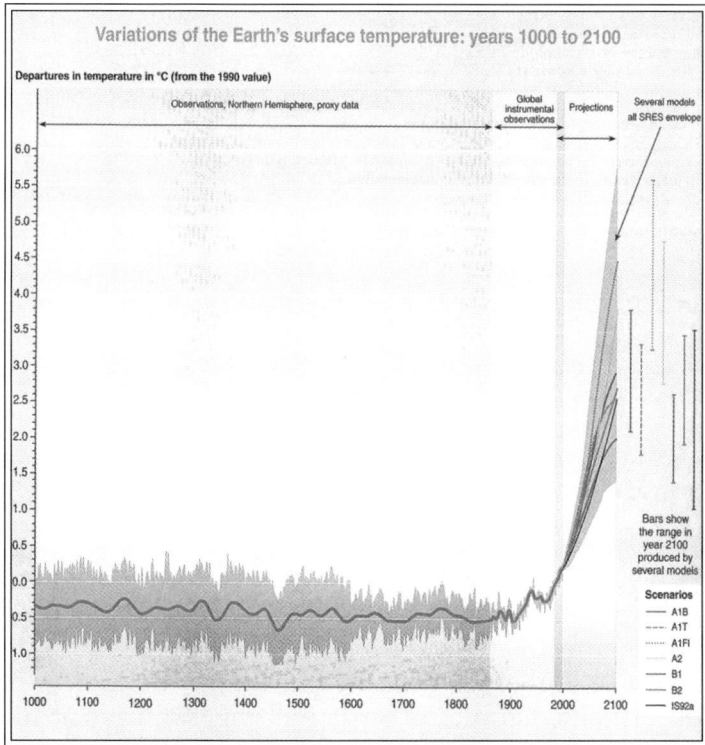

Variations of the Earth's surface temperature: years 1000 to 2100

Departures in temperature in °C (from the 1990 value)

How temperatures have increased recently

Figures 9 and 10 are the only graphs in this book, as I know that non-mathematicians and non-scientists don't like graphs. These two are quite simple to understand. Sometimes you see a temperature graph on a hospital bed showing how the patient's temperature varies over a few days. If all is well, the graph is a nice, smooth, flat curve. If it rises, this should cause some concern, and the steeper the rise the worse is the patient's condition. The figures at the bottom of a patient's graph are simply the days; at the bottom of the graphs in Figures 9 and 10 the figures are the dates. The higher the curve is at any given

FIGURE 10. CO_2 graph (J. Houghton and IPCC, Prince Philip Lecture)

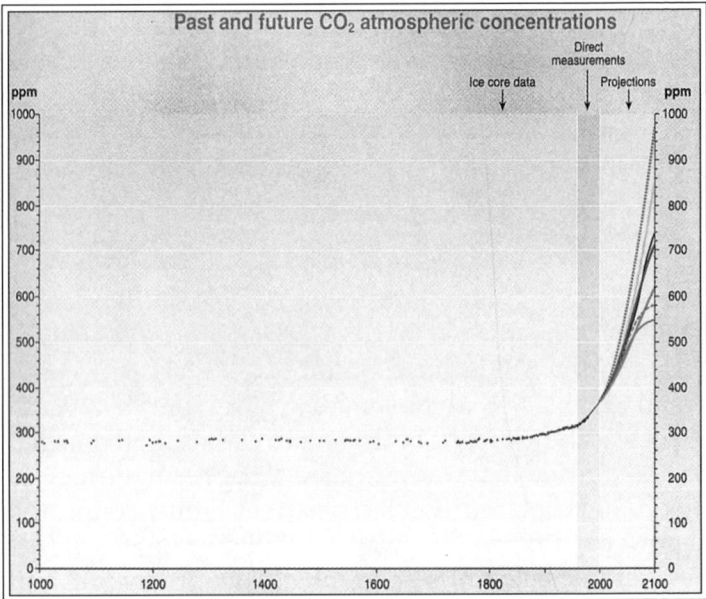

How CO_2 has increased recently

time the higher is the temperature. Of course, the global graph has some ripples and irregularities, and these are probably due to other causes, such as solar activity. But the overall trend is very clear: ever upwards, and faster as we go.

It is interesting – to say the least – to ask why this is so. Around 1800, Europe experienced the stirring of industrial activity that we call the 'Industrial Revolution'. At the root of it lay the discovery that steam power could replace natural sources of energy like horses and water-power. The mills and factories then coming into existence were soon to need power by steam so that much larger machinery could be installed and the buildings also had to be much bigger and stronger. Similarly, the birth (in England) of the public railway system in the 1820s meant that steam locomotives could replace horse-drawn road vehicles and canal boats. By the mid-19th century, Britain, then known as the workshop of the world, had entered the steam age with a vengeance. The trouble was that steam required coal to be burnt, though that was abundantly available from the mines beneath the land and (eventually) sea.

By the middle of that century, new methods had been devised for the manufacture of chemicals on a large scale and also steel. Each, again, required coal. In the case of steel, it was first turned into coke but all processes spewed CO_2 into the air in huge quantities. Later, petroleum began to replace coal for some purposes, but the overall effect was the same. As both contain carbon, both yielded carbon dioxide to the atmosphere. Coal-gas lighting was eventually replaced by electric street lights, connected to power stations miles away but still burning fossil fuel (coal and petroleum). The graph of coal-production and use in the UK is a continuously smooth curve, reaching 28 million tons per annum by 1900.

In the 40 or so years after World War II, there was a veritable explosion in the domestic market. The list of 'must haves' for a typical home included washing machine, fridge and radio. It has been argued by those who don't want to accept global warming, that production of these necessities involved a vast increase in manufacturing and emissions, and this should therefore be reflected in CO_2 levels and temperatures at the time. In fact, CO_2 levels and temperatures did not greatly increase in this period, but those critics fail to realize or admit that these decades were also those of Clean Air Acts and dramatic reduction of domestic fuel burning. Before the war, almost every house in the big cities had a coal fire, but afterwards this became quite a rarity. So the two effects cancelled each other out. Again, coal production statistics confirm simply a steady growth.

The 20th and 21st centuries had to cope with two additional problems of carbon emissions. One was the motor car. Once the pride of only the rich, it soon became essential for every family to have one, especially in the years after World War II. What was once a luxury became a necessity. Cars were needed for shopping, for instance. As a result, supermarkets and other large stores decamped to the outskirts of big towns where customers could readily park their cars. Town centre high streets lost much revenue, many shops closed and other businesses moved away. The social consequences were great, but so was the cost to the environment. Again, cars became essential for the 'school run', and children who had hitherto walked to school (to the great advantage of their health) were now transported to the school gates. In some cases, it became a status symbol to arrive at school in as luxurious a car as possible. In a similar way, churches began to need car parks, and I know of one available church that was never reopened for the simple reason it was surrounded by buildings and there was nowhere for the cars to go.

In 2007, a conference was called in the English Midlands for councils to get together to combat the growing problem of road traffic congestion. The roads bosses, all 11 of them, were summoned to the central meeting. Every single one of them turned up in a car! Even the national press was stirred by this outrage.

When it comes to car design, some vehicles are worse polluters than others. Among the worst are the 4×4 variety. Though designed for rough terrain in the country, they often never leave the town and are noted for their frequent appearance on the notorious 'school run'. All of us need to think very seriously about what kind of cars we buy.

The other scourge of modern times is air travel. The larger the aeroplane the more fuel it will consume and the more CO_2 it will eject. It is quite impossible to appreciate this by watching an airliner gracefully land or take off; its fumes are almost invisible but they are still there. Air travel may only represent a small per-centage of all carbon emissions, but it is the fastest growing emitter. Each year, aircraft throw about 600 million tons of CO_2 into the atmosphere, and if you take just one long flight, say between London and New York, that trip will produce up to 2 tons for you alone, almost certainly more than your car will emit in a whole year, and probably more than you would give off in a lifetime if you simply walked everywhere. Next time you are tempted to take a cheap overseas holiday by air, do think again!

Of course, there are many who defend the airlines. Maybe holidays abroad are a luxury, but not all business trips, surely. Some of these are necessary, but many could be saved by telephone conference calls or email. Other arguments for air travel are its speed, and yet others rest on the economic damage to a nation that does not extend its airports, does not create new runways and would otherwise lose out to less prurient competitors. The opposition, we are told, is determined to set the clock back and return us to a primitive existence. They could be right, for the inexorable climate change is too bad to contemplate.

I know of at least one missionary society that deliberately plans international conferences in remote locations, to make them attractive spots to visit and to ensure as global a mix of delegates as possible. Unfortunately, everyone has to get there by plane, and air miles mount up and are proudly counted. One worker reported for 2 months of 2007 '29,000 miles of ministry travel'! Other Christian societies, to their great credit, limit staff travel to the very minimum and encourage forward planning and group travel by land wherever possible.

What, then, if anything, can be done? We can of course join with my friend in the chemist's shop and forget about it, hoping for the best. But action *can* be taken, on at least six levels!

Action 1. *Taking carbon dioxide out of the air*

We need to take measures to take some of this carbon dioxide out of the air. This chiefly involves immediately halting the cutting down of forests, even if they are on the other side of the world. The destruction in Amazonia is only the most glaring example. We can plant trees in our gardens, and avoid unnecessary cutting down of others. There are also schemes afoot for dissolving the unwanted gas in the oceans, but that will require much more thought and research. Which brings us to our second way forward.

Action 2. Promoting more scientific enquiry

Only in this way will ill-thought opposition be thwarted, and well-meant exaggeration avoided. This involves scientists who have often been seen (quite wrongly) as opponents of Christianity. Some no doubt are, but men like Dawkins speak only for a tiny minority. As one of my old professors never tired of saying, 'Christianity has nothing to fear at the bar of reason, but everything to gain' (G. C. Steward). We desperately need much more research and the defeat of ignorance. At the very least, the world's farmers deserve better forecasts.

Action 3. Alternative sources of energy

We should welcome alternative sources of energy that don't emit any (or much) CO_2. Nuclear power is an obvious answer, though it has many problems, not least of image. The question of disposing of nuclear 'waste' that could last for thousands of years is a real one, as is the possibility of a nuclear reactor being a target for terrorist attack. The use of so-called renewable sources such as wind-power, wave-power, or water-currents is favoured by many. However, apart from the 'visual pollution' of wind-farms, there is all the huge energy used in making wind turbines with their 330 foot masts, of bringing them to site and of laying all the requisite cables. It has been calculated that the energy to make them would add up to their total output for not much less than their expected lifetime of only 25 years! In all these 'renewable' suggestions, there are snags and we often do not know the consequences for wildlife. Each side has vociferous defenders, and Christians are divided on which of these two solutions to support, but neither can be ignored. We probably need both.

Action 4. Decisions by national governments

We must do all we can to ensure that our MPs and others do something positive. In Britain, a lead has already been given by the present government (2007) to promote good environmental policy. From curbing air travel by one means or another, to encouraging individual citizens this must be right. Additionally, good land transport has to be stimulated, with use of railways far more than at present. Taxes on fuel-guzzling cars, and encouragement to use bicycles and buses, are ways in which government can really help. So is the promotion of better industrial practice, cleaner machinery, etc.

Action 5. International agreements

Major meetings have been held at Rio de Janeiro (1991) and at Kyoto, Japan (1997), giving birth to agreements on CO_2 control. Unfortunately, only some countries took part, and the great polluters USA and China did not sign up. Enormous efforts have since been made (e.g. by the British government) to get other nations 'on board', but so far without much success.

Action 6. Individual decisions

This is where you and I come in. It may not seem that our personal efforts will have the slightest global effect: not flying so much, economizing on fuel, turning off the electricity when we don't need it, and so forth. We can, however, try to influence others and especially our governments. Indeed, this is where we all come in. In the UK each of us has been asked to cut our carbon dioxide emissions by 60 per cent by the year 2050. That is some challenge! We are invited to examine our 'carbon footprints', the traces of our lives which show how much carbon dioxide we have emitted. It's a humbling exercise, but all men and women of goodwill for our planet should undertake it.

At a meeting at Westminster recently, while discussing the huge problems of demand versus pollution, I was so struck by a remark by one politician that I wrote it down: 'the only way to square the circle is to change human behaviour'. All honour to that man for his insight; his name was Tony Blair. Changing human behaviour (and values) is one of the things Christianity is all about. For those who follow Jesus Christ, the task ahead of us, as we shall see, is even more imperative.

That is the end of a very long – and difficult – chapter. It may have left you depressed, but that was not its intention. It's also the end of a long drag through the mess that we humans have made of our planet Earth. Now it is our joyous task to see what light the gospel of Jesus Christ throws on all this, and how our every thought and action can be affected and transformed by it. So read on: the prospect is full of hope!

Chapter 6

The Earth is the Lord's

Many of us have had the experience of moving to a new home. If it was one we were renting from someone else we couldn't do much by way of alteration or improvement. That happened to us once, when the house we were buying could not be legally ours for a fortnight because the legal processes were so slow. With the full approval of everyone concerned, we moved in as tenants for these weeks, until formalities had been completed. Then my hammer and drill were rarely out of action! The property was ours, and we could do (almost) what we liked with it.

That is the attitude of many people today. Their bodies are theirs, so they can maltreat them as well as care for them, likewise the houses and land they happen to occupy. So they can ravage or pollute as much as they like because, if the world does not belong to them, it probably belongs to no one else. It's a very easy attitude to take. Today, there is a great swing in the West towards individual liberty and against every outward control. Some fear a police state with 'big brother' keeping an eye on you, others are wary of churches coming out with judgements on everything that is controversial. For people who are 'liberated', 'freedom' means more the right to do as they like than the power to do as they ought. Individual conscience simply doesn't matter for them.

However, it is fortunate that many are now realizing that you just can't live like that, and there are certain things that really are right, and others that are clearly wrong. The morality that comes from the gospel may not yet be theirs, but at least they are getting nearer.

If we turn to the Bible, what do we find about the ownership of planet Earth? Quite a lot! Consider first some of the psalms; these songs celebrate the Earth much more enthusiastically than many of us find comfortable. To some they seem a bit too 'earthy' and not sufficiently 'spiritual' because they speak so much of the created worlds. But what do they tell us?

> The earth is the LORD's, and everything in it, the world, and all who live in it (Ps. 24:1).

> The heavens are yours [God's], and yours also the earth; you founded the world and all that is in it (Ps. 89:11).

In case we should naively suppose that 'earth' means only the dry land, the psalmist goes on to add that 'The sea is his' (Ps. 95:5), and while Psalm 24 proclaims that 'the earth' includes 'everything in it' the writer of Psalm 50 is even more explicit: God says '… every animal of the forest is mine, and the cattle on a thousand hills' (Ps. 50:10). The rest of Scripture leaves us in no doubt as to the ownership of 'our' Earth, and even the apostle Paul goes out of his way to affirm it: 'The earth is the Lord's, and everything in it' (1 Cor. 10:26).

So, what does it mean when we say 'The Earth is the Lord's'? Several things, I believe. First, it is his by right of creation.

God created planet Earth

We all know what it is to enjoy and care for our own belongings like houses and cars, even though we did not actually make them. Things we have made ourselves are even more valued: perhaps a special piece of furniture or needlework, a model of some kind, or a beautiful garden. When we say 'the Earth is the Lord's' it is by virtue of his creating as well as owning it. The Bible could hardly put it more simply, 'The sea is his, for *he made it*, and *his hands formed* the dry land' (Ps. 95:5, italics added).

The role of creation in God's plan is magnificently found on the first few pages of the Bible, especially in Genesis 1. This immensely important passage has been ruined for some by fruitless debates on the precise meaning of 'days', attempts to discover exactly how the various events happened, even by arguments about evolution or the age of the earth. This means the true meaning of the text is obscured by efforts to regard its truth as only scientific, rather than spiritual or theological. Whatever our views, let us agree that here is the true word of God on a subject of colossal importance: the condition of planet Earth. For here is celebrated the very first act of creation by Almighty God. Genesis has much to say to us today.

First, it makes it abundantly clear that this universe was not an accident (as some have chosen to believe) but rather the outcome of the will of God. We are not here by chance, nor is our planet Earth! Then, the first few lines also reveal that the universe is a product of divine action, not a spontaneous coming into being. They also deny the possibility that somehow or other the universe might be a part of God, having a life of its own and even feeling, thinking and planning. The ideas of 'Mother Nature', or of a feminized Earth as in the Gaia theory, do not at all square with Genesis. It is important to say this because many well-meaning folk use the idea of a living or even divine Earth as reason for caring for it. All their noble efforts spring from a false assumption at the start. Pantheism, as it is called, has no place in Christian theology.

In the ancient world, the cosmos was thought to be peopled by gods and semi-gods of all descriptions, but such imaginary beings are conspicuously absent from Genesis. The first readers of Genesis must have had rather a shock. Suppose some were from Egypt. For them the sun was of such blazing importance and dominated so much that they worshipped the sun-god. When the sun in the Genesis story is relegated to day 4, their devotion to it would have been severely challenged. According to this record, creation is the work of *one* God, a belief shared by Christians, Jews and Muslims.

In the New Testament, we read these words, often the high-spot of an English Christmas service of Lessons and Carols:

> In the beginning was the Word, and the Word was with God, and the Word was God. He was with God in the beginning. Through him all things were made; without him nothing was made that has been made. In him was life, and that life was the light of man. The light shines in the darkness, but the darkness has not understood it (John 1:1–5).

The 'Word' here is Jesus, and the passage goes on to tell of his rejection by his own people. Jesus Christ is identified as God and the creator of all things. It points to the great mystery of the Trinity, one God, in three persons, Father, Son and Holy Spirit. The word Trinity is absent from our Bibles, but the idea is there in great abundance. Our small minds may find this hard to understand, and great thinkers have sometimes stumbled at it (not least Isaac Newton). But we can't avoid it if we take Scripture seriously. The early church coined the word 'Trinity' to describe the essence of God. What it means here is that Jesus Christ is God and was involved in the creation of the Earth. It is therefore his own planet Earth that he visited in order to die for us sinful people on the cross.

So, for Christians, there is an even more powerful reason for respecting creation: it is the work of our Lord and Master, Jesus Christ.

There's something else. This creation was created 'good' (see Gen. 1) and, despite our mauling it around, it still can be (see 1 Tim. 4:4). At their creation, 'the morning stars sang together and all the angels shouted for joy' (Job 38:7). It's not that the stars had a voice like ours, or even that they were alive and conscious. Stars do not need to have their 'worship songs', only human beings may want to do that. Rather it is *by being there* that they give praise to God, and that is true of all of nature, including our corrupted planet Earth. By liberating it from its corruption we can restore it to a state where it can again form part of the heavenly chorus and give perfect praise to its Maker.

One of the more engaging TV gardeners (Chris Beardshaw), has admitted that he has often forgotten his lines during filming, but he does his best to get across his love for gardens. He said that for him, they were 'a reflection of paradise on earth', the sort of environment he'd want to spend eternity in. Until Christ returns, our gardens can indeed reflect his glory and be wonderful places to encounter the living Christ. That was the experience of Mary Magdalene early on Easter morning, even 'supposing him to be the gardener'! In the profoundest possible sense she was right, for he *is* the author of all the radiance displayed by flowers, trees and even grass.

You may well object to the Victorian sentiment that we 'are nearer God's heart in a garden than anywhere else on Earth', but surely we can see God's handiwork in nature's wild places: the forests, hills and mountains of the world. In the heyday of Victorian agnosticism, one self-proclaimed agnostic announced of another that 'in the mountains he did feel his faith'. And it is hard to believe that this was not true. The greatness of the mountains dwarfs us into insignificance, and their majesty overwhelms us. At the very least they can help some of us glimpse something of the Creator's love and power.

That is another reason why care of planet Earth is so important. In the 17th century, Francis Bacon – one of the founders of modern science – thought that science could reverse the effects of the Fall and restore nature to its original state. This is now very doubtful, but we can do something by caring for the environment and releasing it to a state nearer to that which God intended. At very least, that means getting rid of pollution and the poisons left behind by our predecessors.

Now to another aspect of a world belonging to God.

God cares for planet Earth

It's sometimes hard to believe that God actually cares for this material world. There is so much suffering, so much ugliness, that we tend to think that we are written off by God. For all that, it is worth remembering that the Bible, sent to a fallen race, offers the most amazing prospect of forgiveness and renewal. Once we see that, a most extraordinary scene comes into view. It is that of the Creator caring for, and even loving, the planet he has made.

Back in early history, there was some kind of cata-clysmic flood that wiped out all who lived in that part of the Earth. When all was over, and the few survivors had been assembled, Almighty God entered into a covenant [agreement with promises] with not only humans but 'all living creatures' (Gen. 9:9,10), and indeed with the physical world, promising both a rainbow (Gen. 9:14) and a maintenance of seasons (Gen. 8:22).

In later years, as Israel developed as a nation, it was given plenty of commands that urged animal welfare, even though, as Hugh Montefiore put it, man is made in the image of God – the beasts are not. So straying and injured animals are to be rescued, an ox must be allowed to feed while working (Deut. 25:4), an animal must be cared for by its owner (Prov. 12:10) and so on. There may have been social reasons for some of these commands but not for all of them, and they certainly show that God cares for 'dumb animals'. So should we, in discussions about battery farming, automated milking, maximizing profit from the management of herds, and the steps taken during epidemics like foot-and-mouth disease.

If you are not persuaded about the value of non-human creation, look at the last seven chapters of the book of Job. We hardly ever read them but today – as then – they have much to say to us. The poor sufferer is drawn from his self-pity by an approaching storm on a really big scale. The Lord speaks to him 'out of the storm' and invites him on a tour of the natural created world. In immense detail we hear of the worlds of thunder, lightning, snow and ice, of the movements of the planets and the constellations. In case Job imagines that *he* set all this up, he is then shown some of the wonders of the animal world, with much detail and not a little humour (the ostrich is extremely fast, but also so daft that she lays her eggs in the ground where any animal may trample on them!). Paraded before Job's eyes is a stream of animals, small and large, culminating in the great and mysterious sea creature whose power is so legendary that no one has ever tamed it. No wonder the poor man stopped his complaints and repented in dust and ashes (see Job 42:6). All was well with him at the end, but he could now understand that God cared for the rest of nature as well as for him.

In the book of Psalms, there are dozens of references to nature. In psalm after psalm we are introduced to a God who is certainly Lord of history, but also Lord of nature. Alan Richardson once remarked that the Jews discovered God was Lord of nature because they had first recognized him as Lord of history, their history in particular. If he did not so passionately care for this material world, why should it be described in such immense and loving detail?

For centuries the Psalms used to be the principal thing sung in churches. Some were in Latin, others in an old (and not very accurate) English translation that had to be sung in special ways, some were versified in metrical form, and some are very modern English renderings. Now, unfortunately, psalms are no longer popular with many congregations. It has often been pointed out that a church that has largely abandoned psalms in its worship is a good prey to paganism. It is also a good prey to environmental carelessness.

When we turn to the New Testament, we see the attitude of God to nature, and we see above all the person of Jesus Christ. In his ministry, Jesus was dealing with the Earth that he had made, tarnished though it had become. His healings were about restoring a little of its former wholeness, and as he broke the bread and fishes before 5,000 hungry people, he was just handling some of his own raw materials. Even when being tested in the desert he retains his command. As Tom Wright has put it, 'From his time with beasts in the wilderness (Mark 1:13) he is now striding through the garden, putting things to rights' (Tom Wright, *Mark for Everyone*, SPCK).

The gospel writers show how news of Jesus' divinity slowly dawned on the people. Mark records how one evening he stilled a sudden squall on the lake where he and his friends were afloat. We read 'He scolded the wind', it died down and the danger was averted. See the Creator Christ rebuking his own creation! His friends in the boat were overcome by great and nameless awe and asked each other: 'Who is this? Even the wind and the waves obey him!' (Mark 4:41). A somewhat similar incident took place later when he amazed his friends by walking on the waters of the lake and bidding the storm subside (see Mark 6:45–52), but this time they could not make anything of it. However, Matthew tells us that eventually those in the boat confessed 'Truly, you are the Son of God' (Matt. 14:13). They did so because they had seen him in action as the Lord of creation.

We human beings find it hard to see how nature could be pleasing to God. In that famous hymn 'Angel voices ever singing' the writer says that 'we know that Thou rejoicest o'er each work of Thine', but by this he seems to mean just the creative activities that God has delegated to man: 'Craftsman's art and music's measure, For Thy pleasure, All combine'.

Like many Victorian writers, he completely failed to mention God's delight over nature itself. We have discovered that he was wrong.

A rejection of some Victorian pietism and pseudo-spirituality, a new understanding of how mechanical the universe seems to be, and many other things have helped us to see in Scripture that God's care for his world was there all the time. This is shown when creation offers an even more powerful incentive for being respected.

God keeps planet Earth in existence

If we recall that, at the moment of creation, God impressed upon nature the scientific laws that continue to this day, we may be tempted to assume that now 'creation' is all over, a thing of the past. This was once a popular view with many peoples, Christian and otherwise. It flourished in the 17th century and was called deism. It accepts that God made the world but denies that he has anything more to do with it. This of course is not the biblical position. As we have seen God is freely at work on planet Earth. But there is an even more important thing to say. In the Old Testament, some deliverances of Israel were clearly due to natural causes (like winds keeping back the waters). These are sometimes called 'interventions', a word much beloved by some Christians today. To think like that, is not to reach the heights of God's involvement with his universe. To suppose that he occasionally intervenes is not what he has said. Because this idea is not far from deism it is sometimes called 'semi-deism', and is a very popular belief today. It explains some things we see as just 'natural' events, but regards those that we cannot explain as acts of God. But it won't do. If these 'acts of God' can one day be understood as 'natural', where is God? He is just a 'god in the gaps'. So what's the alternative?

The position of the Bible is that God is *always* acting in and for his world, whether we think we can understand it or not. This full-blooded theism, as it is called, portrays God as the sustainer of the world. A great passage about Christ makes this plain:

> For by him all things were created: things in heaven and on earth, visible and invisible, whether thrones or powers or rulers or authorities; all things were created by him and for

him. He is before all things, and *in him all things hold together* (Col. 1:16,17, italics added).

An older translation puts the last words 'by him all things consist'; others use the word sustain, but the meaning is clear: through Christ this Earth and the whole universe is kept daily in existence. Another passage says much the same, that 'The Son is ... sustaining all things by his powerful word' (Heb. 1:3).

A simple analogy may help, suggested by Donald MacKay. Imagine you are watching something on TV. It could be a discussion, a play, a concert or even a gig. You watch and enjoy. Then someone suddenly pulls the TV plug out of the socket, the screen darkens and all the good things being watched disappear completely. That's a bit how it would appear to be if Christ were to 'pull the plug', as it were. Instead, this is a world that he sustains moment by moment. It is therefore even more obviously a world for which we should care.

It is very clear that God made, cares for and upholds our material planet Earth. All parts of our planet are aspects of his creation, and show us why we need to care for it. But with some Christians this smacks of materialism, and is miles from their more 'spiritual' goals. That is one reason why they don't like the Psalms! It's also why some Victorian hymn-writers ignored the created world. But, as we have seen, it flies in face of all the Bible's teaching. The distinction between spiritual and material goes back to the ancient Greeks and was much emphasized by medieval theology and since. It should not be allowed to stain our image of a God who made all. William Temple once said that Christianity was the most materialist of all religions. We can and must insist that our care of creation begins to approach that of its Creator.

Chapter 7

Stewardship

'Stewardship' is a most peculiar word. When another book of mine which had a section about 'stewardship' was circulating in America, at least one response that came back to me was this: 'I thought stewardship was just about giving money to the church once a year!' You don't have to only go to the USA to hear that kind of thing. All over the Western world, churches put on a great effort to raise cash for themselves, and their efforts climax in what they choose to call 'Stewardship Sunday'. Have you ever come across that?

Up to a point they are right. Churches *do* need money, and they *do* need to see this is as part of their role in ushering in the kingdom if God. But that kind of stewardship is a small part of a much bigger concept, which is what this chapter is about. It is really the hijacking of a noble word. The word (or related words) is biblical enough and curiously has relations with the Greek word for 'ecology', which in turn comes from the word for 'household', over which a steward has responsibilities.[2]

---

[2] The Greek words are: οικοσ (household), and οικονομοσ (steward). Compare the New Testament word sometimes used for 'earth' or 'world', οικουμενε [= economy].

It means the overseeing of the whole economy of planet
Earth, and doing so on behalf of the Creator God. That
includes maintaining our church buildings, of course,
but also helping to maintain Earth itself – a much taller
order! This stewardly care runs right through the Old
Testament, though the word 'stewardship' (essentially a
Greek one) is of course never used. But it is implied. In
the New Testament we have the same idea, though the
precise word is often linked to even bigger things about
a master's economy and is not limited to care of his land.
Several parables tell how an owner left his possessions
in the care of a steward who may or may not have taken
care of them. The real punch, however, comes in that first
chapter of the Bible, where, as we have seen there is so
much of relevance today.

The old Authorized Version has achieved some
notoriety over its rendering of Genesis 1:26, where human
beings are granted 'dominion' over all living creatures.
This has been taken by some as too authoritarian, too
imperialistic, too demeaning of the rest of creation for
modern tastes. As we shall see, such fears are misplaced,
so let's ask what, according to the Bible, stewardship
actually means.

In case we should imagine that 'stewardship' is a
modern discovery, let us briefly listen to two past voices.
First, John Calvin in 1554:

> The Earth was given to man, with this condition, that he
> should occupy himself in its cultivation ... The custody of
> the garden was given in charge to Adam, to show that we
> possess the things that God has committed to our hands, on
> the condition, that being content with a frugal and moderate
> use of them, we should take care of what shall remain ...
> *Let everyone regard himself as the steward of God in all things*
> *which he possesses.* Then will he neither conduct himself

dissolutely, nor corrupt by abuse those things which God requires to be preserved [italics added].

In a similar way an influential author of the 18th century, Rev. William Derham FRS, assured his readers 'That these things are the gifts of God, they are so many talents entrusted with us by the infinite Lord of the world, a stewardship, a trust reposed in us; for which we must give an account at the day when our Lord shall call'.

One reason why this passage and many others have been neglected is that we have tended to confuse stewardship with self interest. After all, good stewards do also save money!

Yet stewardship is *not* the same as self-sufficiency but has rather bigger tasks in view.

Responsibility

This is a key thought. The parables of Jesus often speak of stewards: the labourers in the master's vineyard (see Matt. 20:1–16), the men with 'talents' (see Matt. 25:14–30) and above all the folk left in charge of a vineyard (see Mark 12:1–9). In every case, these hired workers are seen as *responsible* to the man who selected them. Indeed, that's the point of each story. The parables were all, of course, told to a people who were not expecting Jesus to be crucified, let alone rise from the dead and hold the world to account. Christ shows how wrong they were. When he spoke of their using their 'talents', he wasn't referring to only their natural gifts but also to their *opportunities*, and these are abundant in all kinds of areas, including the environment. We are to use them as people responsible to our King.

Another fact that emerges from a close study of Genesis 1 is that we are made in the image of God (see Gen. 1:27). If so, we cannot act irresponsibly to the universe that he has so carefully and wonderfully made; we must exert 'dominion' in the same benevolent and loving way as he does. He is concerned about detail, about the well-being of people, and care for the poor. Only if we do these things can we be said to be acting responsibly, in the image of our God. Opponents of Christianity have argued vigorously that this text has led to a wholesale exploitation of planet Earth ('ghastly', some of them call the verse). However, many have written of the sceptics' 'desperate exegesis' that leads some to suppose that this is

FIGURE 11. *Punch* magazine cartoon (1935)

The vicar and the gardener

what the verse means. It becomes possible for them only if they forget the words about God's 'image' and that we are all called to act with deep responsibility.

Our responsibility towards our world is amusingly illustrated by a cartoon from *Punch* magazine shown in Figure 11.

A country vicar, dressed and speaking as they did then, is on his rounds. In one front garden he observes a gardener, Wilks, hard at work. He speaks to him:

> VICAR: It's wonderful what the hand of man can do with a piece of earth with the aid of Divine Providence, Wilks.
>
> WILKS: You should 'ave seen this place, sir, when Divine Providence 'ad it all to itself.

Several things are illustrated by this conversation. One is that the Earth, by itself, is in a mess. It isn't even what it once was. From a hot air balloon over England you can see today hundreds of miles of hedging surrounding hundreds of small fields. However, 250 years ago things were very different. From around 1750 there came into being laws called the Enclosure Acts, breaking up vast fields that had existed for centuries, maybe cultivated in strips. Until at least recently, there was an isolated survivor of this in the Great Field near Braunton in North Devon, occupying hundreds of unenclosed acres. The only survivor today seems to be in Laxton, Notts. Several species seem to have been lost by the process of enclosure.

In the case of Scotland, you don't have to go back as far as that. The land was previously pretty barren, but dotted with crofts whose owners managed to eke out a meagre existence on land round their cottages. Then throughout the 19th century came the infamous Highland Clearances where crofters were evicted from their homes, and 'their' land was seized by the big landowners who legally owned it. They had discovered that sheep-farming was more profitable than renting out crofts, so the latter have almost all been swept away.

Clearly, the 'hand of man' has affected the environment, and not in very good ways. So we have here an illustration of how all nature seems to be affected by our sin and stupidity. The Bible shows that creation is affected by our sin. Thus Paul writes in Romans:

> For the creation was subjected to frustration, not by its own choice, but by the will of the one who subjected it, in hope that the creation itself will be liberated from its bondage to decay and brought into the glorious freedom of the children of God.
>
> We know that the whole creation has been groaning as in the pains of childbirth right up to the present time (Rom. 8:20–22).

In part, this may help to explain the tsunamis, earthquakes and other 'natural disasters' that so afflict our world. Many disasters in nature are due to extreme weather conditions, and as we have seen, climate change can be laid at the doors of human activity. We can therefore ask, are these events due to creation being out of sync because of human sin? Would it have been any different before the Fall? The answer must be at least partly so. The growth of AIDS, the effects of smoking, death through drunken driving, etc. are often linked to human failures. To explain everything nasty in that way is a dangerous game, for there is evidence of a violent Earth and a violent animal creation long before man arrived on the scene. That is just a cautionary note, but human ruining of creation is absolutely clear.

There is another aspect to this problem. You see it all around you in uncultivated fields and also on the very high ground of the British Isles. Take Scotland again. Years before our modern times, the Highland tops were covered by trees (not conifers planted by the Forestry Commission between the wars). Oak, ash, alder, etc. grew where now there are only trigonometrical points or layers of snow on the peaks. Very early on, the owners allowed sheep to roam where they would, including the mountain tops. The animals ate the tiny growing new trees and gradually eliminated them. The tops and sides of the great mountains of Scotland (and Northern England) are now bare and inhospitable slopes. The high peaks were no longer places where, as Wilks would say, 'Divine Providence had it all to itself'. In other words, our planet has not only been changed by human activity, but sometimes by our neglect. It may not matter much that Ben Nevis is not crowned by trees any more, but it matters rather more if fields and front gardens are left to thorns and thistles.

Genesis tells us that both women and men have been affected by sin and that nature is involved: God spoke to our first ancestors in Genesis 3:16–19.

Our task as stewards is therefore to work, even by 'the sweat of our brows', to overcome this desolation. And in doing so we shall discover that the vicar was right and it will be 'wonderful what the hand of man can do with a piece of earth with the aid of Divine Providence'. We do not have to leave it to a *Punch* cartoon to tell us that. Whereas the tenants in Jesus' parables were left to themselves (a parable can only teach one or two main lessons), he also told his disciples that 'I will be with you always' in the age following his resurrection. Time and again we are assured that it is God who works with – and in – us as we do his will, not least in looking after the world he has made. That is what makes responsible stewardship a realistic and exciting prospect.

Sustainability

It is here that we come up against a buzzword that always appears in discussions about the environment: sustainability. I confess that when I first heard about 'sustainability' I hadn't any idea what it meant. Gradually, it dawned on me that it was really quite simple. It simply means that we don't go on using resources that will sooner or later dry up, and that we make a choice to use those that can be renewed. Let me give you an example.

In the days before universal central heating, winters in our home were brightened by a huge coal fire. We delighted to sit in front of it and get warm and cheerful. When the children returned in almost Arctic conditions from school, the fire awaited them – it was the focus of our household. We didn't know then, as we do now, that coal is a dirty fuel that send up lots of poisonous substances through the chimney, and helps to develop dense fogs outside. Nor did we know that supplies were getting dangerously low; it was not a freely available resource as we had thought.

All the time, of course, coal fires were emitting copiously carbon dioxide which helped to increase the enhanced greenhouse effect. But then that was true of most other fuels that were burnt, in power stations miles away, or in gas-fired central heating systems. None of these fuels was renewable and we were not sustaining God's Earth.

Now suppose we replaced the coal with wood. To be sure, that still emits CO_2, *but in a sustainable way*. The growing of new trees in our lifetime is possible, and they will take back all or most of the CO_2 and then will be available for fuel again. And so it could go on. Of course nuclear power, for all its problems, is not only sustainable, but also fails to give off CO_2. And wind and wave power offer similarly sustainable solutions. Use of oil and gas for central heating is also unsustainable, as they come from diminishing supplies in the ground. We can always turn off unwanted heaters, and perhaps live at $1°C$ lower than last year and see whether we even notice!

When it comes to fuelling our transport, cars, and worse still, aircraft, are the worst offenders. The supplies of petroleum are also running out and will probably not last much more than the end of the century. Solutions are simple: drive less, and fly as little as possible. Where possible, use bicycles or railways (which are far more efficient in their use of fuel). Don't be like a certain public figure who ostentatiously travelled one way by train – but had his chauffeur meet him at the station with his car which he had driven empty for the same distance! Also, it may be possible one day to replace petrol as a fuel, at least for cars. The alternative is to derive the fuel in some way from biological systems; these may be obtained from the rotting of trees and other plants in the ground and from fermentation. The combustible products may be alcohols or other more complex substances. Together they are called 'biomass' and developments are eagerly awaited. Because of their organic origin they offer another sustainable resource. 'Hydrogen cars' emit only water!

Use of energy resources is the most obvious example of sustainability in practice. But it's by no means the only one. Consider the use of additives in sustainable gardening and farming. Take the use of peat, for example. This is widely dumped on to garden soil but it is in fact a non-renewable resource and supplies are dangerously low. Peat bogs are home to a unique collection of living things and, for some, their last resource. There are now less than 5,000 acres of peat bog in southern England and calls for their destruction must be resisted. Use of peat in gardens is controversial – it is certainly not a nutrient to add to the soil. Moreover, open peat bogs that have been allowed to dry after extraction of the peat emit greenhouse gases and therefore must be kept moist.

Then what do we eat? Take meat, for instance. Consumption of meat per person in the USA is about 112 kg each year. In India, the figure is about 2 kg. Europe is nearer to America than to India, but globally speaking there is not enough meat to go round. Our consumption is therefore unsustainable. Similarly, many old communities have been successfully farming their land for centuries. This includes Amish and Mennonite communities in the USA and many tribes living in the tropical forests. Both systems are sustainable, yet modern threats ranging from new motorways to eviction from native haunts are alike threatening them.

Water is another commodity often in short supply, even in Britain. Don't leave taps running, and be sparing in the use of water in cleaning the car and watering the garden. You must certainly avoid waste, especially of fuel: don't leave unneeded lights on, motors running, even the TV on standby (which uses half as much power as having the TV switched on). Support your local authority in its efforts to recycle waste and minimize the use of rubbish tips. 'Make do and mend' was a motto for World War II and is not a bad one for our present days.

Sustainable living also means being prepared to use things in unorthodox ways. A rather splendid example occurs in 2 Samuel. When the ark was safely carried to Jerusalem, and David the king had prospered, he was pleased to offer oxen in sacrifice to God. But how to make a fire? He was advised, 'Here are oxen for the burnt offering, and here are threshing sledges and ox yokes for the wood' (2 Sam. 24:22).

Finally, good sustainability depends sometimes on getting one's priorities right. It is not always possible to care for the planet in every possible way, so we have to make choices. To give a simple example, we have done our best to encourage wild birds into our garden, blue tits and the like. We now have evidence of a couple of magpies which, we know, are predators and will attack the nests of smaller birds. Each is a product of God's creative hand, yet we can't care for them all. Therefore, I dispel the magpies whenever possible, because my priorities – rightly or wrongly – belong to the smaller birds which they will attack. In passing, I ruefully reflect that we are, magpies and all, part of a fallen universe where full justice is not yet done.

Accountability

After all that has been said, many of us agree that we should be faithful stewards, that we owe it to ourselves, to our descendants and above all to the One who has brought everything into being. And yet we dither and do almost nothing. We are all so busy that we don't want to face yet another challenge. Another day, perhaps? Most of us are past-masters in the art of procrastination – we wouldn't be human if we weren't! Or maybe we feel it's not for us but for the 'professionals' (whoever they may be): people who know about such things more than we do, and have a lot more time and energy. In fact, such enviably situated 'professionals' do not exist, but we invent them as excuses for our own inaction.

In some cases, of course, our own vested interests are at stake, which was the issue for slave-owners in the 19th century. Though they agreed on paper with the abolitionists, they had too much to lose if they liberated their slaves. Only two factors stopped them in their tracks: one was the force of English public opinion and the constant pressures exerted long after 1807 by men like Fowell Buxton. The other was the relentless message of Scripture proclaiming all humans equal before God, a message that inspired Buxton and his friends for 40 long years.

In our case, there are two similar effects. One is that, by all scientific evidence, time is running out. It may well be faster than we think. For example, our climate is rapidly changing and demands instant action. We are accountable to our children and to their children after them. From this point of view alone we have no time to lose.

The other comes back to the Bible. Here we are told of our responsibilities as stewards of God's world; but we also learn something more. That is that our stewardship is accountable to God, and one day we shall be judged for it. All the parables of Jesus on this subject tell us that before he returns to his world, a day of reckoning is coming. The effective steward is rewarded, the timid but well-meaning idler is condemned. In an age when a billion people on this planet are denied pure water, those who are commended are folk who have given a 'cup of cold water' to those who needed it. You can't be more environmental than that!

People sometimes say that 'I personally can make only such a tiny difference that it doesn't matter what I do; I can waste my resources, pollute the air, travel heedlessly by plane, burn all I want, have a generally good time and no one will feel any difference. What does it matter?' Well, listen to what Paul said: 'Now it is required that those who have been given a trust must prove faithful' (1 Cor. 4:2). That is a modern translation. The old AV puts it much more clearly: 'it is required in stewards that a man be found faithful'. That's it! We are required to be *faithful*, not necessarily *successful*. Of course, if everyone is faithful we shall all visibly gain. But if you are the only person in the whole world and are faithful, you will receive your reward, for Jesus Christ loves the individual who turns to him, the 'lost sheep' whom he came to save. So if we hear the King asking us on that day 'what have you done with my world?' each of us will have to give an honest answer. May we be faithful to the end!

Chapter 8

Mission: care of the poor

We have seen two good reasons why we should care for planet Earth: the fact that it is God's, not ours, and the fact that we humans are meant to be stewards. Often in the past that would have been enough. After all, scriptures on the subject are very clear! Yet, on further looking at the Bible we can see there is another, perhaps even more compelling, reason for earth-care. This lies in the call to *mission*.

Every Christian is part of the universal church which Jesus commissioned to 'go and make disciples of all nations'. First the new disciples had to receive baptism, testifying to their repentance and faith in the risen Christ. Then the church was to go, 'teaching them to obey everything I have commanded you' (Matt. 28:20). And that's where we come in.

Making disciples means making learners or followers of the master concerned, in this case Jesus Christ. In other words, the new Christian is to be like his or her Lord as far as possible. To see what that was in practice we can do no better than hear the words of our Lord's first public manifesto. He was in his local synagogue and they handed him a 'roll' of scripture to read from. He unwound the roll till he came to a passage from Isaiah (chapter 61) and he read as follows:

The Spirit of the Lord is on me, because he has anointed me to preach good news to the poor. He has sent me to proclaim freedom for the prisoners and recovery of sight for the blind, to release the oppressed, to proclaim the year of the Lord's favour (Luke 4:18,19).

At this early stage in his ministry, he did not mention his eventual death or rising again. People would never have understood. What he did focus on is of extraordinary interest, however. The reference to 'anointing' suggests a claim to kingship – everyone would have understood that. What follows suggests that his kingship was not as would be expected. It was to be marked by compassion, by care first of all for the poor, the 'don't haves' not the 'must haves' of this world. We may agree with Indira Gandhi who said that 'poverty is the worst pollution'. Without doubt, poor environment leads to poor people.

Then Jesus proclaimed liberty (freedom for the prisoners), healings (of the blind) and a reign of social justice (releasing the oppressed). There was nothing proud or grand, nothing even 'spiritual'. Extraordinary! Then he referred to 'the year of the Lord's favour', an Old Testament instruction which commanded the Israelites to enjoy 'rest' and freedom from grinding labour once every 50 years. Even the land was to 'rest', so nothing was sown or reaped for 12 whole months (see Lev. 25).

Possibly he read further into that chapter of Isaiah – there was plenty more of this kind of material available. However, Luke rather implies not. Jesus had said enough. The mention of the special year would have reminded his hearers of the concern God has for his Earth. More obviously, they would have heard his ringing tones declare the social content of the gospel. Desmond Tutu was reported as saying that those who cannot find social concern in the Bible must be reading a different Bible from his! Here it is, plain for all to see. At the heart of Jesus' first teaching was concern for liberty and social justice and they must be essential components of all true 'mission'.

Anyone who looks at the environment around us must see that much deprivation and suffering is primarily due to social causes: corruption, oppression and so on. These must be put right, but that is not the theme of this book. When it comes to the physical ills of our planet, we have to face the unpleasant fact that it is the poor who suffer first. In the light of Jesus' clear teaching, that is additional reason for doing something to care for our environment. This must never obscure the wonders of salvation and atonement, and it is not a substitute for them. Instead, responsible care for the Earth can be seen as just part of the greater gospel that we treasure – never a substitute for it. But because it is part of our great commission, and because Jesus cares for the poor, we must do so also, and that includes applying all our skills to eliminate pollution and corruption of the Earth. This is not an optional extra – it is part of the faith that should give yet another reason for care of the Earth and should drive Christians to urgent action.

In the rest of this chapter, we shall try to see what needs of the poor can be relieved by responsible care of the environment. They will actually turn out to be needs of us all, it's just that the impoverished feel them first.

Secure homes and shelter

When I went to South America, I had the unusual experience of staying in a 5/6 star hotel (not at my expense, I add!). It was an interesting experience, but shocking in contrast to the shanty town I passed on my way from the airport, for the 'houses' there were hundreds of flimsy structures made of cardboard, old packing cases and whatever else happened to be available. They clung precariously to the sides of the Andes, and people lived in them almost within sight of my hotel. It was an example of social inequality that would have brought condemnation from Christ. But it was also a bad use of Earth's resources and was subject to landslides and all kinds of natural disasters. The shanties showed just how intertwined were the issues of poverty, injustice and the environment. People deserved better than that.

It remains a fact that millions today lack what we Westerners regard as our right, suitable housing. We have seen how subsidence in flooded land as well as encroachment of the desert can render multitudes homeless. So can landslides. In the present century, sea levels are expected to rise by over 20 cm, and this poses a deadly threat to people living in low-lying coastal areas.

This is not just a problem for low-lying territory in Asia, such as Bangladesh, for example. In South America, the coasts, as well as the inland shanties, are likely to be badly affected, particularly in places like Guyana where 600,000 people could suffer. Sea level rises of 1 metre are expected here and in parts of eastern Africa.

It has been calculated that 10 million people are under constant danger from sea level rise. The IPCC reckon that through global warming 'there will be flooding and landslides' which pose the 'most widespread direct risk to human settlements'. If in our lifetime three million people lose their homes from these causes every year, how do we react to the declaration in Isaiah that our duty is 'to share your food with the hungry and *to provide the poor wanderer with shelter,* when you see the naked, to clothe him, and not to turn away from your own flesh and blood' (Isa. 58:7)? Since climate change will be largely responsible, we must do everything possible to halt it. Otherwise we stand condemned.

Not all threats to houses can be laid at the door of climate change, however. There are still plenty of natural disasters for which we may, or may not, be indirectly accountable. Take tsunamis, for instance. There has been widespread criticism of various governments for failing to give adequate warnings of the tsunami that recently originated off the coast of Indonesia. The excuses that it would cost too much sound lame compared to the damage it caused.

Earthquakes are frequently experienced in Japan, often starting with earth slip under the ocean. An official early warning system has been severely condemned for giving grossly inadequate time to evacuate buildings in Tokyo, and described as 'myth sanctioned by government'. In New Zealand, the government and other buildings in Wellington have been entirely reconstructed from wood, rather than heavy stone, and in a manner likely to withstand the worse tremors in the Earth. A Baptist chapel in one town has the printed notice 'In the event of an earthquake the congregation should get under the pews in order to avoid objects falling from the roof'! Such simple advice avoids the need for an expensive early warning system and shows how ordinary citizens can take effective avoiding action.

Similarly volcanic eruptions can often be predicted, but not always.

Fresh water supplies

Water is arguably the most wonderful liquid on Earth, as well as being far and away the most abundant. Without it our life is impossible, so it is not a surprise to read so much about it in the Old Testament. For part of their history, the Israelites were a bunch of ill-disciplined nomads roaming through a howling desert. Small wonder that the provision of water was among the most spectacular of the miracles of Exodus! When, eventually, they reached the Promised Land, water was a continual necessity that could not be taken for granted, and the so-called ' historical books' (Samuel, Kings and Chronicles, and also Nehemiah and Ezra) and the later prophets make much of it as an essential commodity. Yet, as one prophet observed of God, 'The poor and needy search for water, but there is none; their tongues are parched with thirst. But I the LORD will answer them; I, the God of Israel, will not forsake them ...' (Isa. 41:17).

That should be a clarion call for God's people today to do all they can to alleviate the acute global crisis in fresh water, a commodity denied to 1 billion of our fellow humans. British Christians should give a warm approval to the Millennium Goal no. 7 of the Department for International Development, which is to halve the proportion of people worldwide who have no access to safe drinking water and sanitation by 2025.

Adequate food supplies

Next to thirst, the human longing for food is one of our strongest feelings. At the feeding of the 5,000, Jesus told his disciples 'Give them something to eat', a command that proved impossible to obey in those circumstances. In one of the miracles reported by all four Gospel writers, the crowd of 5,000 were fed miraculously at Jesus' command. Today, such demonstrations are much rarer than then, partly because we can do so much for ourselves. Care of planet Earth demands that we give attention to those aspects of our environment that can induce hunger, and to those that can prevent it. Love for our neighbours will mean that they do not starve to death.

First, we must relentlessly fight the spoiling of the Earth that means there is not enough food to go round. In our world, that means above all over-production of food today that will mean many go hungry tomorrow. Over-fishing of the oceans is a classic case, and it is not hard to predict that in a few years' time there will simply not be enough fish to go round. It is noteworthy that the environmentally-conscious nation New Zealand has actually banned all exploitation of 31 sea-havens around its coastline, and hopes to set aside 10 per cent of its coastal waters by 2010. This includes fishing, hunting and all other undesirable spoiling of the marine environment.

Then we face the huge problem of waste, discussed in chapter 4. This partly comes from regulations, and involves ditching mountains of food that is theoretically past its sell-by-date. Such regulations are sometimes very misplaced and need re-examination. Supermarkets cannot be blamed for following the letter of the law. Usually, however, avoidable waste is an individual matter, and each of us must ensure it doesn't happen in our household – easier said than done!

More effective farming can also ensure that food is produced efficiently. In Britain, farmers routinely complain of the mountains of paperwork demanded before they can do their real work. Personal observation suggests that their complaint is all too often justified and pressure is needed from ordinary citizens to cut the 'red tape' to a minimum. Much of this red tape has to do with subsidies, put in place to 'protect' us from 'unfair' or unsubsidized competition from abroad. The same applies to fishing. The European Union is reported to subsidize its members to the extent of £500 million per annum, but even then many trawlers are confined to their east coast ports. Christians have the chance to raise as widely as possible the whole question of food subsidies, though it is a very complicated situation world wide. The environment and politics are inextricably linked.

Ridding crops of disease may involve the death of millions of tiny creatures that cause the problem. Today, pests destroy 50 per cent of crops throughout the world, 70 per cent in the poorer countries, and need to be destroyed. But that should not make us too squeamish, as that kind of choice is part of our world. Every time a vegetarian (or anyone else) swallows a glassful of fresh water, millions of microbial organisms will be destroyed. Does it matter? If, as Jesus taught, we are many times more valuable than even a sparrow, then especially virulent micro-organisms have little right to survive.

The recent outbreak of foot-and-mouth disease in Britain is a good example of official bungling. There was a programme of mass-slaughter which caused animal suffering at the hands of exhausted slaughter men, and destruction of flocks that were many centuries old and somehow 'knew' their territory and where safely to roam. Long-term financial damage was done to farmers (despite some compensation for animals actually destroyed). Then again, compensation was on occasion badly administered, enabling a few farmers to retire on the proceeds. Vaccines were not administered, partly because the UK government was determined to maintain the UK's 'disease-free' status at all times (national pride?), and in 1990 had persuaded its EU partners to adopt a similar policy. As one writer pointed out, such policies put children at risk of exposure to disease and place profit above other virtues. There was *no* public inquiry.

One suggestion is that the poorer countries of the world could gain by the introduction of genetically modified (GM) crops. This, of course, raises a host of moral problems for the Christian (has God given us a right to create new species?). In fact, however, it has been recently shown that it is simply not practicable for GM crops to be used in this way, chiefly on the grounds of cost.

More helpful to the needs of developing countries are the efforts by European Christians to train their poorer colleagues by working on the spot with them. This has been going on for years, perhaps the best-known of the early examples being the ill-fated expedition up the River Niger in 1841, when, as part of Buxton's attempt to abolish slavery in West Africa, it was intended to establish a Western-style hospital. Sadly, the good intentions were frustrated by rampant disease. Since that time, there has been much agricultural work and education in Africa, often today in cooperation with the local churches. Sub-Saharan areas like Chad are already being affected by climate change, Lake Chad once nearly as big as Wales has almost disappeared. Aid is being given in advice for irrigation and sinking of boreholes. The soil, now unstable because of the felling of trees for firewood, has also been a victim of drought. An extensive tree-planting service has been introduced. In nearby Nigeria, similar tree programmes are under way and aid is offered in the processes of animal farming. This has included the rearing of rabbits to augment the farmers' income, and also of chicks as food and for their eggs. The notorious susceptibility of chickens to bird flu has helped in a general programme to encourage the services of trained vets in farming. Crop rotation is rare, because there is often not enough arable land available. So training has been given in the preparation and use of composts. Further to the west, Ghana is yet another country with a regular tree-planting cycle. As always, nomadic tribes are the hardest to help, but efforts are being made. The tale could be continued for the African continent, and of course for many other places as well.

Health

Here again every man and woman has the right to good health, though sadly many fail to enjoy it. Some causes of disease have been touched upon in previous chapters, though those likely to be due to global warming have rightly had most emphasis. Christians today who waste energy, leave lights blazing on when not needed, make needless journeys by air, have little idea that they are helping to enhance the greenhouse effect still more, and that many babies and older people thousands of miles away will suffer. We *must* do all we can to minimize climate change.

Then there is the question of medicines. As reported recently the new anti-malarial drug ASAQ will soon be available in sub-Saharan Africa at realistic prices because its production has deliberately not been restricted to rich drug companies. This has been aided by a medical charity and is a great example of what might be done. Also a more sensible attitude to DDT and similar insecticides is fortunately coming about and needs to be encouraged.

Direct action by Christian organizations has long helped in the treatment of disease. From the days of the earliest missionaries, who established hospitals and clinics in unlikely places, to sophisticated ships that have highly skilled medical and surgical volunteers who are constantly on medical duty at the ports they visit, the Christian church has been in the lead on such provision. This ministry is growing, and much appreciated. In extreme cases, casualties can be flown to Europe for the specialized treatment available only there, and a few small missionary aircraft are available as part of that service or as shorter haul air ambulances.

Our duty to the poor of this world is also shown in the ministry of Christian radio stations. Here there are regular programmes on routine health care and specialist advice is given on matters like AIDS and HIV. Listener responses are regularly analysed and suggest that in many remote areas the signals are being received and the advice taken. This is seen as a part of their ministry for sharing the whole gospel.

Finally, we all need unpolluted environments if we are to survive with even a modicum of good health. Never was this more apparent in Victorian Britain than among factory workers. The following comment was made about 150 years ago, but is still profoundly true. Its author, an alkali manufacturer himself, had seen the effects of a foul atmosphere. He may or may not have had a Christian commitment, but his remarks strike a specially Christian tone:

> To an ordinarily simple-minded individual, it seems neither unreasonable nor unfair that the manufacturer should be pressed to keep his smells and his miscellaneous nuisances to himself. And most men must agree that however little else some of us may be heir to, we have all at least a divine inheritance – if not a prescriptive right – in air and water undefiled. If then the manufacturer – as the embodiment of power – rob the poor man – as the embodiment of weakness – of his oxygen; or dilute that oxygen with deleterious gases and vapours; or if he practically force him to make use of water which he has knowingly contaminated, the injury applies to what is of more value than silver – health. (J. Morrison, Presidential Address 1878–1879, *Trans. Tyne Chem. Soc.*, 1878)

The remarkable thing about these feelings is that they seem to have been genuinely held by a factory-owner whose factory was doing just what he deplored, depriving working people of clean air. It shows, on one hand, how those in power *can* exercise true responsibility. It shows also that to do so may involve much effort and money. It is much the same today.

Chapter 9

The end of the matter

Challenge for today

So we have at last reached the final chapter! It may be useful to summarize the main points in our journey so far.

We have seen that there are three ways in which our environment is under threat. First, there is *pollution* on a huge scale of land, water and air. Then there is the *ravaging* of God's Earth with waste, loss of species and much else to deplore. Above all we have to contend with *climate change*. It so happens that I began writing this final chapter on Easter Monday. That is, three days after the appearance of the second Report for 2007 of the Intergovernmental Panel on Climate Change (IPCC). This was released on Good Friday. It has been produced by top scientists from over 100 countries, and has already been welcomed by the World Health Organization and leading national scientific academies, including Britain's Royal Society.

It gives me no pleasure to state that it is largely in line with chapters 3, 4 and especially 5 of this book. If anything, it makes even more chilling reading, for it confirms that the poor will be the first to suffer badly from the dire effects of global warming, especially in the Arctic region, in sub-Saharan Africa and the mega-deltas of Asia.

However, the temperate zones of the northern hemisphere (where we live) might actually gain short-term from sunnier summers and better harvests. Unsurprisingly, the report has had a cool reception from the White House, and from a few journalists and newspaper editors in the UK who should know much better. Among other effects, it predicts the disappearance of coral reefs and of one quarter of Earth's species by the end of the century. The disappearance of Bolivia's Chacaltaya Glacier is now firmly ascribed to man-made global warming.

Such reflections may cause despair for our environment, and we could fall into a deep pessimism. If things are really as bad as that what hope may there be? This book is trying to argue that there is hope – real solid hope – for the world in the Christian faith, beginning on the first Good Friday. It was on another Good Friday that the climate change report was finalized. Both events offered dreadful warnings to a heedless humanity. Yet each, in very different ways, held out a hope for the future. The day of the crucifixion saw the temple veil (curtain) torn from top to bottom, so indicating the new access to God for mankind, through the death of his Son. The recent Good Friday suggested a much more limited hope, but one that extended to the Earth as a whole. Each Friday, in its own way, was 'Good'. So we may remind ourselves that against the three dreadful threats to our environment may be set three messages of Christian challenge that should motivate all our efforts for the Earth. These were that it *belonged to God*, not us, that it required faithful *stewardship* in its care, and that no account of *Christian mission* was adequate that did not take seriously our responsibility for the world and its inhabitants.

As I have mentioned, this chapter was started on Easter Monday. The morning before, with countless other Christians, I was celebrating Easter Day. In a church full of rejoicing people, magnificent music and a timely reminder that resurrection leaves no space for gloom I was reminded again that Jesus was alive. It was an alarm bell to action. When will we wake up? How much more suffering has to occur before we realize that we are charged to act? We shall not be the first Christians to do so, and in 1992 a meeting at the Au Sable Institute in Michigan led to the establishment of an Evangelical Environmental Network. Two years later, it produced an *Evangelical Declaration on the Care of Creation*. The full text of this may be found in R. J. Berry's book on *The Care of Creation* (InterVarsity Press, 2000), but the five main points are given in Appendix 1.

This *Declaration* is fine, and so is much of the legislation already passed or in course of preparation. Yet one is irresistibly reminded of the situation in Britain 200 years ago. At that time, there were declarations galore, societies against slavery and many campaigns. After much battle, an evangelical MP called William Wilberforce succeeded at last in getting Parliament to pass a bill forbidding a slave trade by all British subjects. That was in 1807, and great was the rejoicing by Wilberforce and his friends in the so-called 'Clapham Sect' (which met in South London and sought to apply biblical principles to public life). The act was both good and necessary, but when the cheering had died down, what happened to the legions of black men and women in slavery to white masters in the Americas? The short answer is 'nothing'! Many people today have been reminded how long it took for the penny to drop after the Act of 1807. Although slave trading had been abolished, slavery itself survived. Slavery in the British colonies continued despite the feelings against it and some hesitant government action. Twenty years later, Wilberforce was ailing and had not long to live. One of his colleagues was Thomas Fowell Buxton, a fellow-evangelical. It was left to

Buxton to mastermind the Act for the Abolition of Slavery in 1833. The long gap of 28 years shows that matters of real public concern can be left untouched without additional spurs to action.

The parallel with today is remarkable. Then, as now, there was some action and much concern. Then, as now, some Christians opted out of the discussion or even supported slavery on the grounds of self-interest bolstered up by dubious biblical exegesis. Then, as now, the question could be raised, why has the church taken such a long time to see that the Bible clearly indicates the equality of all people, and a need to protect the Earth? The old hymn 'The Lord hath yet more truth and light to break forth from his Word' was true then as it is today. We had better be looking!

Hope for the future

There remains the big question: when all is said and done, what is really going to happen? What can be realistically expected for the future of planet Earth? How's it all going to end? In popular thought there have been two general expectations: that it will end with either a bang or a whisper!

The whisper has long been the favourite with science. Millions of years after our time we should expect everything, including the Earth, to cool down, along with the sun and other hot bodies around us. Physics used to offer a 'heat-death' [death of heat] for the whole universe. This was once the opinion of Lord Kelvin, one of the founders of modern physics. He believed that 'the end of this world as a habitation for men or any living creature or plant at present existing in it, is mechanically inevitable'. Quoting Isaiah (51:6) he said 'the earth will wear out like a garment'. He thought the world worked just by mechanical principles, unless God directly intervened. Kelvin was a Christian and knew that God could do things quite apart from science. This may have been why a recently discovered personal note, written when he was a young man and not intended for publication, refers to what he calls 'the prophecy of Peter'. He may have had in mind the famous words of the apostle which suggest anything but a quiet heat-death for the universe:

> But the day of the Lord will come like a thief. The heavens will disappear with a roar; the elements will be destroyed by fire, and the earth and everything in it will be laid bare. Since everything will be destroyed in this way, what kind of people ought you to be? You ought to live holy and godly lives as you look forward to the day of God and speed its coming. That day will bring about the destruction of the heavens by fire, and the elements will melt in the heat. (2 Pet. 3:10–12)

As Peter implied, the marvellous event associated with his fiery picture is the return to the Earth of Jesus Christ, at a time unknown to any man but on God's own timescale. As Peter wrote, 'with the Lord a day is like a thousand years, and a thousand years are like a day' (2 Pet. 3:8). In the last few days before the cross, Jesus went out of his way to tell his disciples about the times of the end. Then he will come again. We read of portents in heaven and on earth, of wars and rumours of wars, of natural disasters (of which we ourselves have seen more than a previous generation), and much else besides. Every Christian needs to live as though Christ will return in his or her natural lifetime. Exactly how the personal return of Jesus relates to much else at the time of the end, including the reconstruction of Earth, has been the subject of countless books and sermons and is hotly disputed by some, often in ignorance of the apocalyptic language of Revelation and other books. It doesn't matter! What we can be certain of is the *fact* of his return, not its *timetable.*

The vastly important thing is that – one day – the Lord of this planet will return to it and at last take it over. The new Earth that he will make will be related to the old familiar one that we inhabit, but it will be free from pain, fear, separation, bereavement and above all from death. From that first Easter Day, death has been conquered, and all who follow Christ can share in his immortality. Not just a few but hundreds of references in Scripture are our guarantee.

So where does this leave our care for the environment? For some Christians it means doing nothing. They think that if Christ will truly restore the Earth, what is the point of their trying to do so? Frequently, this is just an excuse, but not always. It flies in the face of all that Scripture says about stewardship and mission, and is almost a head-in-the-sand closing of eyes to the crying need about us. Rather, I suggest, there are many more helpful attitudes that we can take in the light of the return of our Redeemer.

One is that we must 'maintain the glow'. Our feelings of hope and expectation should increase as we see the Day approaching, and the love we have for our Lord should intensify as we look forward to seeing him at last. Then, we must surely be determined to relieve the plight of others. As Peter showed us, there will be suffering on a huge scale as the Earth becomes increasingly intolerant of the faith, and that suffering will increase, especially of the poor. If we do not ourselves do anything to care for the Planet, we know who is going to suffer. It will be the poor and helpless whom Christ came to save, it will be ourselves as we hang our heads at the judgement seat of Christ, and above all it will be our Lord himself who suffers with his creation. Next, we should remember the terms of our stewardship. In our Lord's parable, it was the one who failed even to try to use his talents who received the worst judgements from the returning master. Finally, we should welcome the King. Often in Scripture, God is seen as entering his temple, to the rapturous applause of the worshippers. They are told to open the gates. We are all familiar with the new 'gates' of railway level-crossings which are rather lifting barriers which, when vertical, permit vehicles to pass through. Something like that must have been in the mind of the psalmist when he cried 'Lift up your heads, O you gates, be lifted up you ancient doors.' The action of the gates was something of a salute as well as a permit. So may our welcome be: 'and the King of Glory shall come in'.

Down the centuries, people have wondered about these things and much else in the gospel of Jesus. Like an American writer, W. Y. Fullerton, they simply cannot understand, for instance, 'why He, whom angels worship, should set his love upon the sons of men'. Who can? Like Fullerton they are also baffled by the prospects before them. However, with him they can affirm upon scriptural evidence and with glowing confidence:

> But this I know, the skies will thrill with rapture,
> And myriad, myriad human voices sing,
> And Earth to Heaven, and Heaven to Earth shall answer.
> At last, the Saviour, Saviour of the world is King!

So, Christ will take over the Earth, still ravaged and polluted as it may be, making in due course a new Earth with a new Heaven. Put plainly, the King will come into his own, for the Earth is his by right. It will be a time of unspeakable joy for those of us who have agonized over the dereliction that our race had caused to the planet and now see it restored to its proper glory, the handiwork of its Creator.

Paul expresses the even greater hope of a reconstruction of this suffering world, picturing creation as waiting 'in eager expectation'. Then, he writes, 'I consider that our present sufferings are not worth comparing with the glory that will be revealed in us' (Rom. 8:18). That is what we look forward to, not a lifeless heat-death.

Therefore, we need to work at the environment as though everything depends on us; and yet to pray and expect as though everything depends on God! Both are true for all work proclaiming the good news. Meanwhile, the presence of the risen Christ among his people – even before his bodily return – will enable them to accomplish so much that would otherwise have been impossibly difficult for them. His resurrection means that, if his ideals are followed, and his power used by his disciples, many new people will find new life in him through faith. Till then his gospel encourages us to pray and work so that the world can be vastly improved, until that day when it will be gloriously remade. That is our prospect, that is our hope.

Appendix 1

The Evangelical Declaration on the Care of Creation

(Main points only; full statement in R. J. Berry's book *The Care of Creation*, InterVarsity Press, 2000)

1. As followers of Jesus Christ, committed to the full authority of the Scriptures, and aware of the ways we have degraded creation, we believe that biblical faith is essential to the solution of our ecological problems.

2. We and our children face a growing crisis in the health of the creation in which we are embedded, and through which, by God's grace, we are sustained. Yet we continue to degrade that creation.

3. Many concerned people, convinced that environmental problems are more spiritual than technological, are exploring the world's ideologies and religions in search of non-Christian spiritual resources for the healing of the earth. As followers of Jesus Christ, we believe that the Bible calls us to respond in four ways [which are then enumerated].

4. Thus we call on all those who are committed to the truth of the gospel of Jesus Christ to affirm the following principles of biblical faith and to seek ways

of living out these principles in our personal lives, our churches, and society [ten 'principles' are then listed].

5. We believe that in Christ there is hope, not only for men, women and children, but also for the rest of creation which is suffering from the consequences of human sin.

Appendix 2

Books you may find helpful

Barclay, Oliver, *Thomas Fowell Buxton and the Liberation of Slaves*, Sessions, York, 2001.

This is not directly related to the environment, but the parallel between attitudes to the environment and to slavery are clear; indeed the author additionally describes Buxton as 'something of an environmentalist'.

Berry, R. J. (ed.), *The Care of Creation: Focusing Concern and Action*, IVP, London, 2000.

A collection of essays by experts and other well-known people; contains the *Evangelical Declaration*.

Berry, R. J. (ed.), *When Enough is Enough*, IVP, London, 2007.

Another collection of recent essays, covering 'science, agriculture, economics and biblical theology'.

Gnanakan, K., *God's World: a Theology of the Environment*, SPCK, 1999.

Evangelical in outlook, but quite hard work to read!

Houghton, J., *The Search for God: Can Science Help?* Lion, Oxford, 1996; rev. edn, 2007.

An excellent introduction to general issues by one of the Christian pioneers of climate science.

Jones, J., *Jesus and the Earth*, SPCK, London, 2003.

La Trobe, S., *Climate Change and Poverty*, Public Policy Paper, TearFund, London, 2002.

Very clear and relevant; pulls no punches!

Lovegrove, R., *Silent Fields: the Long Decline of a Nation's Wildlife*, Oxford University Press, Oxford, 2007.

A new book that explores how wildlife has been persecuted in the UK, and shows how much our planet has been ravaged near at home.

Moltmann, J., *God in Creation. An Ecological Doctrine of Creation*, SCM, 1985.

Difficult for non-theologians, but very influential and challenging. It had to be included.

Montefiore, Hugh, *Preaching For Our Planet*, Mowbray, 1992.

A series of sermons for the ordinary churchgoer, and a quite early example of such writing.

Prance, G. T., *Earth Under Threat*, Wild Goose, Glasgow, 1996.

Russell, Colin A., *The Earth, Humanity and God*, UCL Press, 1994.

A fuller book by the present author – rather heavier and more academic. The 1993 Templeton Lectures at Cambridge.

Russell, Colin A. (ed.), *Chemistry, Society and Environment, A New History of the British Chemical Industry*, Royal Society of Chemistry, Cambridge, 2000.

Several chapters, e.g. by W. A. Campbell, cover the vast range of pollution introduced by this industry.

Schaeffer, F. A., *Pollution and the Death of Man: the Christian View of Ecology*, Hodder & Stoughton, London, 1970.

A classic in its day, but still with some valuable things to communicate.

Spencer, N. and White, R., *Christianity, Climate Change and Sustainable Living*, SPCK, London, 2007.

Written with the support of the Jubilee Centre, John Ray Initiative, TearFund and others.

Van Dyke, F., Mahan, D. C. Sheldon, J. K. and Brand, R. H., *Redeeming Creation: the Biblical Basis for Environmental Stewardship*, IVP, Illinois, 1996.

An early and collective account.

There are also many papers from journals of considerable merit, far too numerous to be mentioned individually here, but with one exception. That is:

John Houghton, *Climate Change and Sustainable Energy*, the Prince Philip Lecture at the Royal Society of Arts, 11 May 2005.

Appendix 3

Some useful addresses

A Rocha – Christians in Conservation

British branch of an international consortium, concerned with application of Christian principles in action.

3 Hooper Street, Cambridge CB1 2N2

Phone: 01387 710286

email: international@arocha.org

website: www.arocha.org

Au Sable Institute of Environmental Studies

7526, Sunset Trail N.E. Mancelona, MI 49659, USA

phone: (0231) 587 8686 fax: (0231) 587 5353

email: administration@ausable.org

website: www.ausable.org

Established in 1979 and with other centres in the New World and elsewhere. American counterpart to JRI.

Christian Ecology Link

Interdenominational organization, founded 1981; publishes Bulletin and Magazine. Works especially in churches.

20 Carlton Road, Harrogate, North Yorkshire HG2 8DD

phone: 01423 871616
email: cel2000@Christian-ecology.org.uk

Christians in Science (CiS)

The oldest – and largest – group of Christians who are scientists in the UK. Their journal, published jointly with the Victoria Institute, is *Science and Christian Belief.*

Rev. Tom Moffat (membership sec.)
The Manse, Kirk Street, Culross, Fife KY12 8JD or

Dr. Caroline Berry (sec.)
4 Sackville Close, Sevenoaks, Kent TN13 3AD

phone: 01383 880 231 [Moffat] or 01732 451 907 [Berry]

email: cberry@pncl.co.uk
website: www.cis.org.uk

Department for International Development (DFID)

A government department concerned to fight world poverty. It publishes a range of materials, including an excellent free magazine, *Developments.*

DFID
1 Palace Street, London SW1E 5HE;
and
Abercrombie House, Eaglesham Road, East Kilbride, Glasgow G75 4EA

phone:
0845 300 4100; and from overseas +44 1355 843 132

email: enquiry@dfid.gov.uk
website: www.dfid.gov.uk

John Ray Initiative (JRI)

An organization concerned with the application of sound scientific and theological principles to problems relating to the environment. It is named after John Ray, an

English naturalist (1628–1705) who was deeply concerned to apply his Christian faith to creation. JRI was formed in the 1990s by Sir John Houghton, now its president. It publishes four-page *Briefings* on a variety of topics, including climate change, GM crops, and biodiversity. Full list from the office.

Francis Close Hall, University of Gloucestershire, Swindon Road, Cheltenham, GL50 4AZ.

phone: 01242 543 580 fax 01242 532 997

email: jri@glos.ac.uk
website: www.jri.org.uk

TearFund

Formerly *The Evangelical Alliance Relief* Fund. Publishes a wide range of materials especially on poverty and disaster management, as well as on climate change.

100 Church Road, Teddington, Middlesex, TW11 8QE

phone: 020 8943 7818 fax: 020 8943 3594

email: py@tearfund.org
website: www.tearfund.org